Show Singapore Flower

Singapore Flower Show, 1884-1900

Show Singapore Flower
Singapore Flower Show, 1884-1900
ISBN/EAN: 9783337321475
Printed in Europe, USA, Canada, Australia, Japan
Cover: Foto ©ninafisch / pixelio.de

More available books at **www.hansebooks.com**

SCHEDULE

OF THE

FLOWER SHOW

TO BE HELD IN

THE BOTANICAL GARDENS,

ON

THURSDAY AND FRIDAY,

the 10th and 11th January, 1884.

OPEN ON THE FIRST DAY FROM 3 P.M. UNTIL DARK.

OPEN ON THE SECOND DAY
- From 6 A.M. until 10 A.M.
- ,, 3 P.M. ,, 6 P.M.
- ,, 9 P.M. ,, 11.30 P.M.

—:0:—

ADMISSION.

First Day, $1 each person.

Second Day, { 25 cents to 6 P.M.
{ 50 ,, evening.

Ticket to admit 1 person to the whole Exhibition,...$1.50.
Family Ticket to admit 5 persons to the whole Exhibition,...$3.50.
Schools and Charitable Institutions will be admitted free on the second day by an order of the Honorary Secretary, for which application must be made four days previously.

SINGAPORE:
PRINTED AT THE GOVERNMENT PRINTING OFFICE.
[Price, 20 Cents.]

COMMITTEE.

The Hon'ble C. J. Irving, C.M.G.

The Hon'ble Captain McCallum, R.E.

Edwin Koek, Esq.

The Hon'ble E. E. Isemonger.

J. C. F. George, Esq.

G. T. Addis, Esq.

E. Ritter, Esq.

H. Hinnekindt, Esq.

D. Low, Esq.

Tso Peng Lung, Esq.

C. Stringer, Esq.

James Miller, Esq.

H. A. Y. Whampoa, Esq.

Tan Keng Swee, Esq.

N. Cantley, Esq.

R. W. Hullett, Esq.

T. Irvine Rowell, Esq., M.D.,
Honorary Treasurer.

E. E. Everett, Esq.,
Honorary Secretary.

Rules.

1. The competition shall be open to all residents in Singapore, Penang, Malacca, and the Native States.

2. All articles exhibited for competition shall have been grown by the Exhibitor, or must have been in his possession at least four weeks before the day of Exhibition, Bouquets excepted.

3. It is distinctly understood that all flowering plants are to be in flower, and all fruits and vegetables fit for use. The plants in all classes which contain more than one kind, to be dissimilar kinds, except in classes Nos. 16 and 43.

4. All articles included in any entry must be arranged, and the Exhibitors and Assistants must leave the shed by 10 A.M., on the first day of the Exhibition, except Exhibitors in Section III, who will be allowed to remain until 12 o'clock. Plants in pots must be sent in before 5 P.M. the day before the opening day.

5. The arrangement of the productions shall be subject to the direction of the Committee, except in Classes Nos. 16 and 43.

6. The Committee will appoint Judges, from whose decision there shall be no appeal.

7. The Judges will have authority to withhold the prize when they are of opinion that there is not sufficient merit to justify an award; or to award special prizes for anything not mentioned in the Schedule.

8. No Exhibitor shall be awarded two prizes in the same class.

9. Intending Exhibitors must give notice to the Honorary Secretary, at least 10 days before the day of the show, in what

RULES,—*Continued*.

classes they intend to exhibit, and stating the space they are likely to require; otherwise their productions may be rejected. On giving this information, they will receive a numbered card, which must be attached to the exhibits in lieu of the Exhibitor's name.

10. No articles included in any entry shall be removed from the shed before the close of the show. Exhibitors will receive a ticket, marked with a number corresponding to that of their Entries, which must be produced at the close of the show before Exhibits can be removed.

If Exhibitors will carefully attend to the Rules and Notes, and also label their productions with the numbers of the classes in which they wish them to be shown, confusion and dissatisfaction will be avoided on the day of the show.

All reasonable care will be taken of articles while at the show, and plants will be watered.

Should there be a surplus after paying the necessary expenses, accounts for cartage will be considered.

PRIZE LIST. SECTION I.

No. of Class.	Classes.	Prizes.	
		First. $	Second. $
1	**Ornamental Foliage Plants.** Best collection of 20 Crotons in pots or tubs not exceeding 18 in. diam., (Prize given by Baboo S. P. Chatterjee, Calcutta.)	15	5
2	Best collection of 12 Crotons in pots or tubs 9 in. diam..	6	3
3	,, specimen Croton (best grown) in pot or tub not exceeding 24 in. diameter,	5	
4	,, collection of 12 rarest Crotons in pots not exceeding 6 in. diam.,	10	5
5	,, collection of 10 Caladiums,	5	3
6	,, ,, ,, 5	4	2
7	,, ,, ,, 24 Plants,	4	2
8	,, ,, ,, 6 rarest Palms,	3	2
9	,, ,, 12 Ferns,	6	3
10	,, ,, 6 ,,	3	2
11	,, ,, 3 ,,	2	1
12	,, specimen Fern,	3	
13	,, Tree Fern,	2	

PRIZE LIST. SECTION I,—Contd.

No. of Class.	Classes.	Prizes. First. $	Second. $
	Ornamental Foliage Plants,—Contd.		
14	Best collection of 12 Mosses (Selaginella),	5	3
15	,, ,, ,, 6 ,, ,, ...	3	1.50
16	,, ,, ,, not less than 12 nor more than 24 plants arranged for effect, ...	10	3
17	,, collection of 12 Begonias, ..	5	3
18	,, ,, ,, 6 ,, ...	3	1.50
19	,, ,, ,, 3 ,, ...	2	1
20	,, specimen Begonia. ...	1	0.50
21	,, collection of 6 Dieffenbachias,	3	2
22	,, ,, 3 ,, ...	2	1
23	,, collection of 6 Anthuriums. ...	3	2
24	The rarest Exotic Plant, ...	2	
25	,, ,, Native Plant, · ...	2	

N.B.—Exhibitors are requested to note that the plants in all classes which contain more than one must be dissimilar kinds.

Each pot must not contain more than one plant, except in the case of Annuals.

PRIZE LIST. SECTION II.

No. of Class.	Classes.	Prizes.	
	Plants in Pots, in Flower.	First. $	Second. $
26	Best 4 Gloxinias,	3	2
27	,, 2 ,,	2	1
28	,, 4 Geraniums,	3	2
29	,, 2 ,,	1.50	1
30	,, 4 Petunias,	3	2
31	,, 2 ,,	2	1
32	,, 6 Dianthus (Pinks),	2	1
33	,, 4 Verbenas,	3	2
34	,, 2 ,,	2	1
35	,, 4 Antirrhinum (Snapdragon),	2	1
36	,, 2 ,,	1	0.50
37	,, 6 Roses,	5	3
38	,, 3 ,,	2.50	1
39	,, specimen Rose,	2	1
40	,, 6 Orchids,	3	2
41	,, 3 ,,	2	1
42	,, specimen Orchid,	2	1

PRIZE LIST. SECTION II,—Contd.

No. of Class.	Classes.	Prizes.	
		First. $	Second. $
	Plants in Pots, in Flowers,—Contd.		
43	Best group of 24 pots arranged for effect,	10	3
44	12 Annuals (not including Phlox),	2	1
45	,, 6 ,,	1	0.50
46	6 Gladioli,	3	1.50
47	3 ,,	2	1
48	,, 12 Phloxes, ...	3	2
49	,, 6 ,,	1	0.50
50	,, 3 Lilies,	2	1
51	,, 3 Pancratiums,	2	1
52	,, 3 Amaryllis,	2	1
53	,, 3 Gesniraceæ,	2	1
54	,, 3 Dahlias,	3	1.50
55	6 Asters,	2	1
56	,, 4 Chrysanthemums.	3	1.50
57	The rarest Plant,	3	2

N.B.—The Plants in this section must be *in flower* when exhibited. In all classes which contain more than one, the Plants are to be dissimilar kinds. No pot to contain more than one plant, except in the case of Annuals.

PRIZE LIST. SECTION III.

No. of Class.	Classes.	Prizes. First.	Second.
	Cut Flowers.	$	$
58	Best 4 Dahlias, dissimilar,	2	1
59	,, 4 Roses, ,,	2	1
60	,, 3 Chrysanthemums, dissimilar,	1.50	1
61	,, collection of Cut Flowers arranged for effect,	5	2
62	,, collection of Wild Flowers and Ferns named.	3	.1
63	,, Hand Bouquet,—Prize: A Silver Bouquet Holder.		

N.B.—In classes 58, 59, 60 the quantities specified are not to be exceeded; otherwise the Exhibitor will be disqualified.

Exhibitors to provide their own vases, stands, or whatever they exhibit Cut Flowers in.

Flowers in Hand Bouquets must be tied together for carrying, and not arranged loosely in Vases.

In class 62 the specimens should be exhibited fresh, in water, and should have been collected by the Exhibitor only.

PRIZE LIST. — SECTION IV.

No. of Class.	Classes.	Prizes.	
	Vegetables.	First. $	Second. $
64	Best 6 Carrots, ...	2	1
65	„ 3 Cucumbers, ...	2	1
66	„ 3 Lettuces, ...	2	1
67	„ 20 Pods of French Beans, ...	1.50	1
68	„ 12 Onions or Shallots, ...	1.50	1
69	„ 12 Radishes, long, ...	1	0.50
70	„ 12 „ round, ...	1	0.50
71	„ 6 Tomatoes, ...	2	1
72	„ 2 Cabbages, ...	2	1
73	„ 2 Vegetable Marrows, ...	1	0.50
74	„ Bunch of Parsley, ...	1	0.50
75	„ Collection of Native Vegetables, ...	3	1.50
76	„ „ „ Pot Herbs, ...	2	1
77	„ 12 Sweet Potatoes, white, ...	2	1
78	„ 12 „ „ red, ...	2	1
79	„ 6 Capsicums, ...	1	0.50
80	„ 3 Stalks of Celery, ...	3	2
81	„ Bunch of Watercress, ...	1	0.50
82	„ 3 Beet-roots, ...	2	1
83	„ Collection of European Vegetables,	10	5
84	„ „ „ Native „	5	3
85	„ 6 rarest medicinal plants grown in the Colony, ...	5	3
86	„ 6 rarest plants used for texture, ...	5	3

N.B.—Carrots and Radishes should be washed and only a portion of their tops should be left on, say about six inches, all the loose outer leaves being trimmed off.

Cabbages and Lettuces should have their roots and outer leaves trimmed off.

PRIZE LIST. SECTIONS IV & V.

No. of Class.	Classes.	Prizes.	
		First. $	Second. $
	Section IV.—Fruit.		
87	Best 2 Melons,	1	0.50
88	,, 2 Pumelows,	1	0.50
89	,, 2 Pine Apples,	1	0.50
90	,, 2 Durians,	1	0.50
91	,, Bunch of Plantains.	1	0.50
92	,, Dish of 12 Oranges,	2	1
93	,, ,, ,, 12 Mangosteens,	2	1
94	,, Collection of Fruits,	4	2
95	,, 3 Custard Apples,	1	0.50
	Section V.—Miscellaneous.		
96	Best 6 Tapioca Roots,	1	0.50
97	,, 6 Roots of Arrowroot,	2	1
98	,, 6 ,, ,, Ginger,	2	1
99	,, ,, ,, ,, Turmeric,	2	1
100	,, 6 Cocoa-nuts, ripe,	1.50	1
101	,, 6 Cocoa fruits (Cacao),	2	1
102	,, 12 Nutmegs,	2	1
103	,, sample of Pepper, fresh,	2	1
104	,, ,, ,, Cloves,	2	1
105	,, ,, ,, Arabian Coffee,	2	1
106	,, ,, ,, Liberian Coffee,	2	1
107	,, ,, ,, Sugar Cane,	1	0.50
108	,, Ornamental Stand of local make to hold 6 to 9 flower pots,	4	2
109	,, 3 Flower Pots, of local make.	3	1.50

N.B.—Entries in the above must be accompanied by a certificate that the articles have been grown, made, or designed by the Exhibitor.

In classes 103 to 107 a catty of each article is the specified amount for a sample.

In classes 108 and 109 the articles may be labelled with the names of the Exhibitors.

PRIZE LIST

OF THE

FLOWER SHOW

TO BE HELD IN

The Botanical Gardens,

ON

WEDNESDAY AND THURSDAY,

The 29th and 30th July, 1885.

OPEN ON THE 1ST DAY FROM 3 P.M. UNTIL DARK.

OPEN ON THE 2ND DAY
- From 6 A.M. until 10 A.M.
- „ 3 P.M. „ 6 P.M.
- „ 8 P.M. „ 11 P.M.

ADMISSION.

FIRST DAY, $1 EACH PERSON.

SECOND DAY,
- 20 cents before 6 P.M.
- $1 evening.

Ticket to admit one person to the whole Exhibition ... $1.50
Family Tickets   do.   do.   3.00

Schools and Charitable Institutions will be admitted free on the 2nd Day by an order of the Honorary Secretary, for which application must be made 4 days previously. Tickets will also be given free for distribution among Market Gardeners.

Singapore:
PRINTED AT "THE SINGAPORE AND STRAITS PRINTING OFFICE."

COMMITTEE.

—:0:—

SKINNER, HON. A. M.—*Chairman.* ⎱
HULLETT, R. W., ESQ.   *Of the*
KOEK, E., ESQ.   *Garden's*
MCCALLUM, HON. MAJOR H. E.   *Committee.*
MILLER, J., ESQ. ⎰

ADDIS, G. T., ESQ.
CANTLEY, N., ESQ.
GEORGE, J. C. F., ESQ.
GRAHAM, HON. J.
HINNEKINDT, H., ESQ.
IBRAHIM INCHE.
ISEMONGER, HON. E. E.
MAHOMED AL SAGOFF, SYED.
RETTICH, DR.
RITTER, E., ESQ.
SEAH, HON. SEAH LEANG.
STRINGER, E., ESQ.
TAN KENG SWEE, ESQ.
TSE PENG LUNG, ESQ.
WHAMPOA, H. A. Y., ESQ.

Honorary Secretaries.

CANTLEY, N., ESQ.
ISEMONGER, HON. E. E.

Honorary Treasurer.

ROWELL, DR. T. J.

Rules.

—:o:—

1. The competition shall be open to all residents in Singapore, Penang, Malacca, and the Native States.

2. All articles exhibited for competition shall have been grown by the exhibitor, or must have been in his possession at least four weeks before the day of exhibition—Bouquets and Table Decorations excepted.

3. It should be distinctly understood that all plants exhibited in Section II. must be in flower, and fruits and vegetables must be fit for use. The plants in all classes which contain more than one kind, must be dissimilar kinds, except in class 58.

4. All articles included in any entry must be arranged, and the Exhibitors and Assistants must finally leave the shed by 6 p.m. on the day before the Exhibition opens—except Exhibitors in Sections IV., V. and VI., and class 58 who will be allowed to remain until 10 a.m. on the day of opening. Plants in pots cannot be received later than noon the day before the opening day.

5. The arrangement of the exhibits shall be subject to the direction of the Committee.

6. The Committee will appoint Judges, from whose decision there shall be no appeal.

7. The Judges will have authority to withhold the prize when they are of opinion that there is not sufficient merit to justify an award; or to award special prizes for anything not mentioned in the Schedule.

8. No Exhibitor shall be awarded two prizes in the same class, or more than five prizes in the same Section.

RULES,—*Continued.*

9. Intending Exhibitors must give notice to the Honorary Secretary, at least five days before the day of the show, in what classes they intend to exhibit, and must state the space they are likely to require, otherwise their productions may be rejected. On giving this information they will receive numbered cards, which must be attached to the exhibits in place of the Exhibitor's name.

10. No articles included in any entry shall be removed from the shed before the close of the show. Exhibitors will receive a ticket, marked with a number corresponding to that of their exhibits, which must be produced at the close of the show before they can be removed.

If Exhibitors will carefully attend to the Rules and Notes, and also label their productions with the numbers of the classes in which they wish them to be shown, confusion and trouble will be avoided.

All reasonable care will be taken of articles while on exhibition.

Should there be a surplus after paying the necessary expenses, it is hoped that the Committee may be enabled to defray some portion of the cartage.

The co-operation of the community is essential if the show is to be a success.

SECTION I.—Ornamental Foliage Plants in Pots.

In awarding prizes in this Section the flowers of any Exhibits will not be considered.

Class.	Kinds.	No. to be exhibited.	Prizes. First.	Second.
			$	$
1	Panax or Aralia	4	1	...
2	Coleus	6	3	2
3	,,	specn.		...
4	Crotons	12	4	3
5	,,	6	3	2
6	,,	specn.	3	...
7	Maranta and Calathea	6	4	2
8	,, ,,	3	3	1
9	,, ,,	specn.	2	1
10	Palms	3	2	...
11	Caladiums	6	3	2
12	,,	specn.	2	...
13	Dieffenbachias	3	2	...
14	,,	specn.	1	...
15	Aroids other than the above (Pothos, Scindapsus, Alocasia, Colocasia, Anthurium, &c.)	6	3	1
16	,, ,, ,,	specn.	3	...
17	Dracæna	3	2	...
18	Ferns	12	4	3
19	,,	6	2	1
20	,,	specn.	2	...
21	Aliantum Farleyense	specn.	2	...
22	Tree Fern	specn.	2	...
23	Selaginellas	6	3	1
	,, ,, ,, ,,	specn.	1	...
24	Ornamental foliage plants not included in the above	3	2	...
25	,, ,,	specn.	1	...

SECTION II.—Plants in Pot, in Flower.

Class.	Kinds.	No. to be exhibited.	Prizes.	
			First.	Second.
			$	$
26	Pansy	specn.		
27	Dianthus (Pink)	4	2	1
28	,, ,,	specn.	1	
29	Camellia	specn.	2	1
30	Geranium	specn.	1	
31	Balsam	4	1	
32	Rose			2
33	,,	3		
34	,,			
35	Asters	3	2	1
36	,,	specn.	1	
37	Chrysanthemum	3	2	1
38	,,	specn.	1	
39	Dahlia	specn.	1	
40	Phlox		2	1
41	Petunias	3	2	1
42	,,			
43	Antirrhinum	3	1	
44	Gloxinia	4	4	2
45	,,	specn.	2	
46	Other Gesneraceæ (Gesnera, Tyddea, Achimenes, Episcia, &c.)	3	$	1
47	,, ,,	specn.	1	
48	Verbena	3	1	
49	,,	specn.	1	
50	Orchids		5	3
51	,,		3	1
52	,,	specn.	3	
53	Gladiolus	specn.	2	1
54	Amaryllids and Lilies (Crinum Pancratium, Eucharis, &c.)..	4	4	2
55	,, ,,	specn.	2	
56	Collection of Annuals	6	3	1
57	Plant in Flower not included in the above	specn.	1	

SECTION III.—Plants in Pots, whether in Flower or not.

Class.	Kinds.	No. to be exhibited.	Prizes. First.	Second.
			$	$
58	Group of Plants, arranged for effect in space not exceeding 9 feet square	...	5	3
59	Collection of different Plants	24	5	3
60	Begonias	12	4	2
61	,,	6	3	1
62	,,	3	2	...
63	Collection	specn.	2	...
64	Cactus	specn.	1	
65	The rarest Native Plant	...	2	...
66	,, Exotic ,,	...	2	

SECTION IV.—Cut Flowers.

Class.	Kinds.	No. to be exhibited.	Prizes.	
			First.	Second.
			$	$
67	Camellia	specn.	1	...
68	Roses	4	2	1
69	,, ...	specn.	1	...
70	Aster	specn.	1	...
71	Chrysanthemums	3	1	...
72	Dahlias	3	1	
73	,, ...	specn.	1	
74	Collection of Cut Flowers, arranged for effect		5	2
75	Collection of Wild Flowers, arranged for effect... ...		2	1
76	Hand Bouquet	Silver Bouquet holder.		
77	Bridal ,, (White Flowers)	Do.		
78	Table decoration	Do.		

SECTION V.—Vegetables.

Class.	Kinds.	No. to be exhibited.	Prizes. First. $	Second. $
79	Carrots	6	2	...
80	Cucumbers	4	2	1
81	Brinjal	4	2	...
82	Lettuces	4	5	2
83	French Beans	20 pds.	2	...
84	Peas	20 „	2	...
85	Onions or Shallots	12	3	1
86	Radishes	12	1	...
87	Tomatoes	12	5	2
88	Cabbages	2	2	1
89	Vegetable Marrows	2	2	1
90	Sweet Potato (Kledi)	12	1	...
91	„ „ (Yam)	12	1	...
92	Celery	3 stalks.	2	1
93	Beet-root	3	2	1
94	Collection of European Vegetables		10	5
95	Collection of Native Vegetables	...	10	5

N.B.—The Committee are particularly anxious to encourage the Exhibition by Market-gardeners of Native Vegetables and Fruit, and will be prepared to award several Prizes in Classes 95 and 108.

SECTION VI.—Fruits.

Class.	Kinds.	No. to be exhibited.	Prizes.	
			First. $	Second. $
96	Melons	2	2	1
97	Oranges	12	3	...
98	Limes (including Lemons and Citron)	12	2	
99	Pumelows	2	1	...
100	Pine Apples	3	2	1
101	Durians	2	2	1
102	Plantains (different sorts)	...	2	1
103	,, (one bunch)	...		
104	Mangosteens	12	2	1
105	Sour Sop	3	1	...
106	Custard Apple	3	1	...
107	Chiku	2	1	...
108	Collection of Fruit	...	3	1

SECTION VII.—Miscellaneous.

Class.	Kinds.	No. to be Exhibited.	Prizes.	
			First. $	Second. $
109	Tapioca Roots...	6	1	...
110	Arrowroot	6	1	...
111	Ginger Roots...	6	1	
112	Turmeric	6	1	...
113	Cocoa-nuts (ripe)	6	1	...
114	Cacao Fruits	6	1	...
115	Nutmegs	12	1	...
116	Sugar Cane		1	
117	Pepper, sample of fresh		1	...
118	Arabian Coffee		1	
119	Liberian Coffee		1	...
120	Fibres locally prepared from local Plants...	...	3	...
121	Ornamental Flower Stand of local make to hold from 6 to 9 pots	...	2	1
122	Flower Pots (Earthenware), local make	...	2	1
123	Flower Tubs (Wood), local make	...	2	1
124	Collection of Chinese Plants, in pots, of fantastic shape...		3	...

PRIZE LIST
OF THE
FLOWER SHOW
TO BE HELD IN
THE BOTANICAL GARDENS,
ON
TUESDAY AND WEDNESDAY,
THE 15TH AND 16TH JUNE, 1886.

Open on the 1st Day from 3 p.m. until Dark.

Open on the 2nd Day { From 6 a.m. until 10 a.m.
" 3 p.m. " 6 p.m.
" 8 p.m. " 11 pm.

ADMISSION.

FIRST DAY, $1 EACH PERSON.

SECOND DAY, ... { 20 cents before 6 p.m.
{ $1 Evening

Ticket to admit one person to the whole Exhibition ... $1.50
Family Tickets   do.   do.   ... $3.00

Schools and Charitable Institutions will be admitted free on the 2nd Day by an order of the Honorary Secretary, for which application must be made 4 days previously. Tickets will also be given free for distribution among Market Gardeners.

Singapore:
PRINTED AT THE "SINGAPORE AND STRAITS PRINTING OFFICE."

COMMITTEE.

Hon. J. T. Dickson. }
R. W. Hullett, Esq. } The Garden's
E. Koek, Esq.   } Committee.
Hon. Major McCallum, r.e.
J. Miller, Esq.

A. Currie, Esq.
J. G. Davidson, Esq.
Datu Bintara Dalam of Johore.
J. C. F. George, Esq.
H. Newton, Esq.
Hon. F. E. Isemonger.
H. C. Johnston, Esq.
Ven. Archdeacon Meredith, m.a.
Dr. Rettich.
E. Ritter, Esq.
Hon. Seah Liang Siah.
Syed Mahomed Bin Alsagoff.
Syed Omar.
Toe Peng Lung, Esq.
H. A. Y. Whampoa, Esq.

Honorary Secretaries.

N. Cantley, Esq.
C. Stringer, Esq.

Honorary Treasurer.

Dr. Rowell.

Rules.

1. The competition shall be open to all residents in Singapore, Penang, Malacca, and the Native States.

2. All articles exhibited for competition shall have been grown by the exhibitor, or must have been in his possession at least four weeks before the day of exhibition—Bouquets and Table Decorations excepted.

3. It should be distinctly understood that all plants exhibited in Section II. must be in flower, and fruits and vegetables must be fit for use. The plants in all classes which contain more then one kind, must be dissimilar kinds, except in class 48.

4. All articles included in any entry must be arranged, and the Exhibitors and Assistants must finally leave the shed by 6 p.m. on the day before the Exhibition opens—except Exhibitors in Sections IV., V. and VI., and class 48 who will be allowed to remain until 10 a.m. on the day of opening. Plants in pots cannot be received later than noon the day before the opening day.

5. The arrangement of the exhibits shall be subject to the directions of the Committee.

6. The Committee will appoint Judges, from whose decision there shall be no appeal.

7. The Judges will have authority to withhold the prize when they are of opinion that there is not sufficient merit to justify an award ; or to award special prizes for anything not mentioned in the Schedule.

8. No Exhibitor shall be awarded two prizes in the same class, or more then five prizes in the same Section.

RULES—*Continued.*

9. Intending Exhibitors must give notice to the Honorary Secretary, at least five days before the day of the show, in what classes they intend to exhibit, and must state the space they are likely to require, otherwise their productions may be rejected. On giving this information they will receive numbered cards, which must be attached to the exhibits in place of the Exhibitor's name.

10. No articles included in any entry shall be removed from the shed before the close of the show. Exhibitors will receive a ticket, marked with a number corresponding to that of their exhibits, which must be produced at the close of the show before they can be removed.

If Exhibitors will carefully attend to the Rules and Notes, and also label their productions with the numbers of the classes in which they wish them to be shown, confusion and trouble will be avoided.

All reasonable care will be taken of articles while on exhibition.

SECTION I.—Ornamental Foliage Plants in Pots.

In awarding prizes in this Section the flowers of any exhibits will not be considered.

Class.	Kinds.	No. to be exhibited.	Prizes.	
			First.	Second.
			$	$
1	Panax or Aralia	4	1	...
2	Coleus	6	3	2
3	,,	specn.	1	...
4	Croton	6	3	2
5	,,	specn.	3	...
6	Maranta and Calathea	6	4	2
7	,, ,,	specn.	2	1
8	Palms	3	2	...
9	Caladiums	6	3	2
10	,,	specn.	2	...
11	Dieffenbachias	3	2	...
12	Aroids other than the above (Pothos, Scindapsus, Alocasia, Colocasia, Anthurium, &c.)	6	3	1
13	,, ,,	specn.	3	...
14	Dracœna	3	2	...
15	Ferns	12	4	2
16	,,	6	4	2
17	,,	specn.	4	...
18	Adiantum	6	4	2
19	Tree Fern	specn.	2	...
20	Selaginellas	6	3	1
21	Ornamental foliage plants not included in the above	3	2	

SECTION II.—Plants in Pot, in Flower.

Class.	Kinds.	No. to be exhibited.	Prizes. First.	Second.
			$	$
22	Pansy	specn.	2	1
23	Dianthus (Pink)	4	3	1
24	Camellia	specn.	3	1
25	Geranium	3	3	1
26	Balsam	6	2	1
27	Rose	6	4	2
28	,,	3	3	1
29	,,	specn.	2	1
30	Asters	3	3	1
31	Chrysanthemum	3	3	1
32	Dahlia	3	2	1
33	Phlox	6	3	1
34	Petunias	3	3	1
35	Antirrhinum	3	2	1
36	Gloxinia	4	4	2
37	,,	specn.	2	1
38	Other Gesneraceæ (Gesnera, Tydea, Achimenes, Episcia, &c.)	3	3	1
39	Verbena	3	3	1
40	Orchids	6	5	2
41	,,	3	3	1
42	,,	specn.	3	1
43	Gladiolus	3	3	1
44	Amaryllids and Lilies	4	4	2
45	,, ,,	specn.	2	...
46	Plant in Flower not included in above	specn.	3	...
47	Best collection of plants in flower not less than	12	10	

SECTION III.—Plants in Pots, whether in Flower or not.

Class.	Kinds.	No. to be exhibited.	Prizes. First.	Second.
			$	$
48	Group of Plants, arranged for effect in space not exceeding 9 feet square	...	5	3
49	Collection of different Plants	24	5	3
50	Begonias	12	4	2
51	,,	6	3	1
52	,,	3	2	...
53	Cactus	3	2	...
54	The rarest Native Plant	...	2	...
55	,, Exotic ,,	...	2	...

SECTION IV.—Cut Flowers.

Class.	Kinds.	No. to be exhibited.	Prizes. First. $	Second. $
56	Camellia	specn.	2	1
57	Roses	4	3	1
58	,,	2	3	1
59	Aster	3	2	1
60	Chrysanthemums	3	3	1
61	Dahlias	3	2	1
62	Collection of Cut Flowers, arranged for effect		5	2
63	Collection of Wild Flowers, arranged for effect	...	3	1
64	Hand Bouquet		4	1
65	Bridal ,, (White Flowers)		4	1
66	Table decoration	...	4	1

SECTION V.—Vegetables.

Class.	Kinds.	No. to be exhibited.	Prizes. First. $	Second. $
67	Carrots	6	2	1
68	Cucumbers	4	2	1
69	Brinjal	4	2	...
70	Lettuces	4	2	1
71	French Beans	20 pds.	2	1
72	Peas	20 ,,	2	1
73	Onions or Shallots	12	2	1
74	Radishes ...	12	2	1
75	Tomatoes ...	12	2	1
76	Cabbages	2	2	1
77	Vegetable Marrows	2	2	1
78	Sweet Potato (Kledi) ...	12	1	...
79	,, ,, (Yam) ...	12	1	...
80	Celery	3 stalks.	2	1
81	Beet-root	3	2	1
82	Collection of European Vegetables	...	10	5
83	Collection of Native Vegetables	...	5	2

SECTION VI.—Fruits.

Class.	Kinds.	No. to be exhibited.	Prizes.	
			First.	Second.
			$	$
84	Melons	2	2	1
85	Oranges	12	2	1
86	Limes (including Lemons and Citron)	12	2	1
87	Pumelows	2	2	1
88	Pine Apples	3	2	1
89	Durians	2	3	1
90	Plantains (different sorts)		2	1
91	Mangosteen	12	2	1
92	Sour Sop	3	2	1
93	Custard Apple	3	2	1
94	Chiku	2	2	1
95	Collection of Fruit		3	1

SECTION VII.—Miscellaneous.

Class.	Kinds	No. to be exhibited.	Prizes. First. $	Second. $
96	Tapioca Roots...	6	1	...
97	Arrowroot	6	1	...
98	Ginger Roots	6	1	...
99	Turmeric	6	1	...
100	Cocoa-nuts (ripe) ...	6	1	
101	Cacao Fruits	6	1	...
102	Nutmegs	12	1	
103	Sugar Cane	...	1	...
104	Pepper, sample of fresh ...	...	1	
105	Arabian Coffee	...	1	
106	Liberian Coffee	...	1	...
107	Tea	...	1	...
108	Fibre locally prepared from local Plants	...	5	...
109	Ornamental Flower Stand of local make to hold from 6 to 9 pots		2	1
110	Flower Pots (Earthenware), local make	...	2	1
111	Flower Tubs (Wood), local make	...	2	1
112	Collection of Chinese Plants, in pots, of fantastic shape ...	...	2	...

PRIZE LIST

OF THE

FLOWER SHOW

TO BE HELD IN

THE BOTANICAL GARDENS,

ON TWO DAYS TO BE FIXED HEREAFTER

IN

APRIL, 1887.

Open on the 1st Day   from 3 p.m. until Dark.
Open on the 2nd Day { From 6 a.m. until 10 a.m.
                        ,,   3 p.m. ,,   6 p.m.
                        ,,   8 p.m. ,, 11 p.m.

ADMISSION.

FIRST DAY...   ... $1 EACH PERSON.
SECOND DAY   ... { 20 cents before 6 p.m.
                              { $1 Evening.

Ticket to admit one person to the whole Exhibition $1.50
Family Tickets   do.   do. $3.00

     Schools and Charitable Institutions will be admitted free on the 2nd Day by an order of the Honorary Secretary, for which application must be made four days previously. Tickets will also be given free for distribution among Market Gardener.

C. STRINGER,
N. CANTLEY,
Honorary Secretaries.

Singapore:
PRINTED AT THE "SINGAPORE AND STRAITS PRINTING OFFICE."

Rules.

1. The competition shall be open to residents in Singapore, Penang, Malacca, and the Native States.

2. All articles exhibited for competition shall have been grown by the exhibitor, or must have been in his possession at least four weeks before the day of exhibition—Bouquets and Table Decorations excepted.

3. It should be distinctly understood that all plants exhibited in Section II. must be in flower, and fruits and vegetables must be fit for use. The plants in all classes which contain more then one kind, must be dissimilar kinds, except in class 48.

4. All articles included in any entry must be arranged, and the Exhibitors and Assistants must finally leave the shed by 6 p. m. on the day before the Exhibition opens—except Exhibitors in Sections IV., V. and VI., and class 48 who will be allowed to remain until 10 a.m. on the day of opening. Plants in pots cannot be received later than noon the day before the opening day.

5. The arrangement of the exhibits shall be subject to the directions of the Committee.

6. The Committee will appoint Judges, from whose decision there shall be no appeal.

7. The Judges will have authority to withhold the prize when they are of opinion that there is not sufficient merit to justify an award; or to award special prizes for anything not mentioned in the Schedule.

8. No Exhibitor shall be awarded two prize in the same class, or more then five prizes in the same Section.

RULES—*Continued.*

9. Intending Exhibitors must give notice to the Honorary Secretary, at least five days before the day of the show, in what classes they intend to exhibit, and must state the space they are likely to require, otherwise their productions may be rejected. On giving this information they will receive numbered cards, which must be attached to the exhibits in place of the Exhibitor's name.

10. No articles included in any entry shall be removed from the shed before the close of the show. Exhibitors will receive a ticket, marked with a number corresponding to that of their exhibits, which must be produced at the close of the show before they can be removed.

If Exhibitors will carefully attend to the Rules and Notes, and also label their productions with the numbers of the classes in which they wish them to be shown, confusion and trouble will be avoided.

All reasonable care will be taken of articles while on exhibition.

SECTION I.—Ornamental Foliage Plants in Pots.

Class.	Kinds.	No. to be exhibited.	Prizes.	
			First	Second.
			$	$
1	Panax or Aralia	4	1	...
2	Coleus	6	3	2
3	,,	specn.	1	...
4	Croton	6	3	2
5	,,	specn.	3	...
6	Maranta and Calathea	6	4	2
7	,, ,,	specn.	2	1
8	Palms	3	2	...
9	Caladiums	6	3	2
10	,,	specn.	2	...
11	Dieffenbachias	3	2	...
12	Aroids other than the above (Pothos, Scindapsus, Alocasia, Colocasia, Anthurium, &c.)	6	3	1
13	,, ,, ,,	specn.	3	...
14	Dracæna	3	2	...
15	Best collection of adiantum, Ferns, without restriction as to number,		10	5
16	Best collection of Ferns excluding adiantum without restriction as to number.		10	5
17	Specimen Fern		4	...
18	Tree Fern	specn.	2	...
19	Selaginellas	6	3	1
20	Ornamental foliage plants not included in the above	3	2	

SECTION II.—Plants in Pot, in Flower.

Class.	Kinds.	No. to be exhibited.	Prizes.	
			First.	Second.
			$	$
22	Pansy		2	1
23	Dianthus (Pink)		3	1
24	Camellia		3	1
25	Geranium		3	1
26	Balsam		2	1
27	Zinnia		4	2
28	Rose		3	1
29	,,	specn.	2	1
30	Asters		3	1
31	Chrysanthemum		3	1
32	Dahlia		2	1
33	Phlox		3	.1
34	Petunia		3	1
35	Antirrhinum		2	1
36	Gloxinia		4	2
37	,,	specn.	2	1
38	Other Gesneraceœ (Gesnera, Tyddea, Achimenes, Episcia, &c.)		3	1
39	Verbena		3	1
40	Gaillardia		5	2
41	Orchids		3	1
42	,,	specn.	3	1
43	Gladiolus		3	1
44	Amaryllids and Lilies		4	2
45	,, ,,		2	...
46	Plant in Flower not included in above	specn.	3	...
47	Best collection of different Plants in flower not less than	12	10	0

For all classes in this Section, except class 47 and those denoted as specimens, the number of exhibits is not restricted, but in awarding prizes the judges will take into consideration the quantity as well as the quality of each exhibit.

SECTION III.—Plants in Pots, whether in Flower or not.

Class.	Kinds.	No. to be exhibited.	Prizes. First.	Second.
			$	$
48	Group of Plants, arranged for effect in space not exceeding 9 feet square ...		5	3
49	Collection of different Plants	24	5	3
50	Best collection of Begonias ...	...	10	5
51	Specimen Begonia ...		3	2
52	Cactus ...	3	2	
53	The rarest Native Plant ...	...	3	
54	,, Exotic ,, ...		2	...

SECTION IV.—Cut Flowers.

Class.	Kinds.	No. to be exhibited.	Prizes.	
			First.	Second.
			$	$
56	Camellia	specn	2	1
57	Roses	4	3	1
58	,,	2	3	1
59	Aster	3	2	1
60	Chrysanthemums	3	3	1
61	Dahlias	3	2	1
62	Collection of Cut Flowers, arranged for effect		5	2
63	Collection of Wild Flowers, arranged for effect		5	2
64	Hand Bouquet		4	1
65	Bridal ,, (White Flowers)		4	1
66	Table décoration		4	1

SECTION V,—Vegetables.

Class.	Kinds.	No. to be exhibited.	Prizes. First.	Second.
			$	$
67	Carrots	6	2	1
68	Cucumbers	4	2	1
69	Brinjal	4	2	1
70	Lettecus	4	2	1
71	French Beans	20 pds.	2	1
72	Peas	20 ,,	2	1
73	Onions or Shallots	12	2	1
74	Radishes	12	2	1
75	Tomatoes	12	2	1
76	Cabbages	2	2	1
77	Vegetable Marrows	2	2	1
78	Sweet Potato (Kledi)	12	1	...
79	,, ,, (Yam)	12	1	...
80	Celery	3 stalks.	2	1
81	Beet-root	3	2	1
82	Collection of European Vegetables	...	10	5
83	Collection of Native Vegetables		5	2

SECTION VI.—Fruits.

Class.	Kinds.	No. to be exhibited.	Prizes. First.	Prizes. Second.
			$	$
84	Melons	2	2	1
85	Oranges	12	2	1
86	Limes (including Lemons and Citron)	12	2	1
87	Pumelows	2	2	1
88	Pine Apples	3	2	1
89	Durians	2	3	1
90	Plantains (different sorts)	...	2	1
91	Mangosteen	12	2	1
92	Sour Sop	3	2	1
93	Custard Apple	3	2	1
94	Chiku	2	2	1
95	Collection of Fruit		3	1

SECTION VII.—Miscellaneous.

Class.	Kinds.	No. to be exhibited.	Prizes.	
			First.	Second.
			$	$
96	Tapioca Roots...	6	1	...
97	Arrowroot	6	1	...
98	Ginger Roots ...	6	1	...
99	Turmeric	6	1	...
100	Cocoa-nuts (ripe)	6	1	...
101	Cacao Fruits ...	6	1	...
102	Nutmegs	12	1	
103	Sugar Cane		1	
104	Pepper, sample of fresh		1	
105	Arabian Coffee		1	...
106	Liberian Coffee		1	...
107	Tea	...	1.	...
108	Fibre locally prepared from local Plants ...		5	...
109	Ornamental Flower Stand of local make to hold from 6 to 9 pots	...	2	1
110	Flower Pots (Earthenware), local make		2	1
111	Flower Tubs (Wood), local make		2	1
112	Collection of Chinese Plants, in pots, of fantastic shape ...	...	2	

PRIZE LIST

OF THE

TO BE HELD IN

THE BOTANICAL GARDENS,

ON FRIDAY THE 12TH AND SATURDAY THE 13TH APRIL, 1889.

Open on the 1st Day from 3 p.m. until Dark.
Open on the 2nd Day
{ From 6 a.m. until 10 a.m.
    „ 3 p.m. „ 6 p.m.
    „ 8 p.m. „ 11 p.m.

ADMISSION.

FIRST DAY... $1 EACH PERSON.
SECOND DAY ... { 20 cents before 6 p.m.
    { $1 Evening.

Ticket to admit one person to the whole Exhibition $1.00
Family Tickets   do.   do. $3.00

    Schools and Charitable Institutions will be admitted free on the 2nd Day by the order of an Honorary Secretary, for which application must be made four days previously. Tickets will also be given free for distribution among Market Gardeners.

H. N. RIDLEY,
C. STRINGER,
Honorary Secretaries.

Singapore:
PRINTED AT THE "SINGAPORE AND STRAITS PRINTING OFFICE."

Rules.

1. The competition shall be open to residents in Singapore, Penang, Malacca, and the Native States.

2. All articles exhibited for competition shall have been grown by the exhibitor, or must have been in his possession at least four weeks before the day of exhibition—Bouquets and Table Decorations excepted.

3. It should be distinctly understood that all plants exhibited in Section II. must be in flower, and fruits and vegetables must be fit for use. The plants in all classes which contain more than one kind, must be of dissimilar kinds, except in class 50.

4. All articles included in any entry must be arranged, and the Exhibitors and assistants must finally leave the shed by six p.m. on the day before the Exhibition opens—except Exhibitors in Sections IV., V. and VI., and class 50 who will be allowed to remain until 10 a.m. on the day of opening. Plants in pots cannot be received latter than noon the day before the opening day.

5. The arrangement of the exhibits shall be subject to the directions of the Committee.

6. The Committee will appoint Judges, from whose decision there shall be no appeal.

7. The Judges will have authority to withhold the prize when they are of opinion that there is not sufficient merit to justify an award; or to award special prizes for anything not mentioned in the Schedule.

8. No Exhibitor shall be awarded two prizes in the same class, or more then five prizes in the same Section.

RULES—*Continued.*

9. Intending Exhibitors must give notice to the Honorary Secretary, at least five days before the day of the show, in what classes they intend to exhibit, and must state the space they are likely to require, otherwise their productions may be rejected. On giving this information they will receive numbered cards, which must be attached to the exhibits in place of the Exhibitor's name.

10. No articles included in any entry shall be removed from the shed before the close of the show. Exhibitors will receive a ticket, marked with a number corresponding to that of their exhibits, which must be produced at the close of the show before they can be removed.

If exhibitors will carefully attend to the Rules and Notes, and also label their productions with the numbers of the classes in which they wish them to be shown, confusion and trouble will be avoided.

All reasonable care will be taken of articles while on exhibition.

Section I.--Ornamental Foliage Plants in Pots.

CLASS.	KINDS.	No. to be exhibited.	PRIZES.	
			First	Second
			$	$
1	Panax or Aralia	4	1	...
2	Coleus	6	3	2
3	,,	specn.	1	...
4	Crotons	6	3	2
5	,,	specn.	3	...
6	Maranta and Calathea	6	4	2
7	,, ,,	specn.	2	1
8	Palms ...	3	2	...
9	Caladiums	6	3	2
10	,,	specn.	2	...
11	Dieffenbachias	3	2	...
12	Aroids other than the above (Pothos, Scindapsus, Alocasia, Colocasia, Anthurium, &c.) ...	6	3	1
13	,, ,, ,,	specn.	3	...
14	Dracænas	3	2	...
15	Ferns ...	12	10	5
16	,, ...	6	7	3
17	,, ...	3	5	2
18	Specimen Fern	...	4	...
19	Tree Fern	specn.	2	...
20	Selaginellas	6	5	2
21	,,	3	3	1
22	Ornamental foliage plants not included in the above	3	2	...

Section II.—Plants in Pots, in Flower.

Class.	Kinds.	No. to be exhibited.	Prizes.	
			First.	Second.
			$	$
23	Pansies		2	1
24	Dianthus (Pink)		3	1
25	Camellias		3	1
26	Geraniums		3	1
27	Balsams		2	1
28	Zinnias		4	2
29	Roses		3	1
30	,,	specn.	2	1
31	Asters		3	1
32	Chrysanthemums		3	1
33	Dahlias		2	1
34	Phlox		3	1
35	Petunias		3	1
36	Antirrhinums		2	1
37	Gloxinias		4	2
38	,,	specn.	2	1
39	Other Gesneraceæ (Gesnera, Tydea, Achimenes, Episcia, &c.)		3	1
40	Verbenas		3	1
41	Gaillardias		3	1
42	Orchids	6	10	4
43	,,	specn.	4	2
44	,,	Rarest	3	...
45	Gladioli		3	1
46	Amaryllids and Lilies		4	2
47	,,		2	
48	Plant in Flower not included in above	specn.	3	
49	Best collection of different Plants in flower not less than	12	10	0

For all classes in this Section, except classes 42 and 49 and those denoted as specimens, the number of exhibits is not restricted, but in awarding prizes the judges will take into consideration the quantity as well as the quality of each exhibit.

SECTION III.—Plants in Pots, whether in Flower or not.

Class.	Kinds.	No. to be exhibited.	Prizes.	
			First.	Second.
			$	$
50	Group of Plants, arranged for effect in space not exceeding 9 feet square		5	3
51	Collection of different Plants..	24	5	3
52	Begonias	12	10	5
53	,,	3	5	2
54	,,	specn.	3	2
55	Cacti	3	2	
56	The rarest Native Plant		3	
57	,, Exotic ,,		2	

SECTION IV.—Cut Flowers.

Class.	Kinds.	No. to be exhibited.	Prizes.	
			First. $	Second. $
58	Camellias	specn.	2	1
59	Roses ...	4	3	1
60	,,	2	3	1
61	Asters...	3	2	1
62	Chrysanthemums	3	3	1
63	Dahlias	3	2	1
64	Collection of Cut Flowers, arranged for effect		5	2
65	Collection of Wild Flowers, arranged for effect		5	2
66	Hand Bouquet		4	1
67	Bridal ,, (White Flowers)		4	1
68	Table decoration		4	1

SECTION V.—Vegetables.

Class.	Kinds.	No. to be exhibited.	Prizes. First.	Second.
			$	$ c.
69	Carrots	6	1	0 50
70	Cucumbers	4	1	0 50
71	Brinjal	4	1	0 50
72	Lettuces	4	1	0 50
73	French Beans	20 pds.	1	0 50
74	Peas	20 ,,	1	0 50
75	Onions or Shallots	12	1	0 50
76	Radishes	12	1	0 50
77	Tomatoes	12	1	0 50
78	Cabbages	2	1	0 50
79	Vegetable Marrows	2	1	0 50
80	Sweet Potato (Kledi)	12	1	
81	,, (Yam)	12	1	
82	Celery	3 stalks.	1	0 50
83	Beet-root	3	1	0 50
84	Artichokes	6	1	0 50
85	Collection of European Vegetables	...	5	2 00
86	Collection of Native Vegetables		3	1 00

SECTION VI.—Fruits.

Class.	Kinds.	No. to be exhibited.	Prizes.	
			First. $	Second. $
87	Melons	2	2	1
88	Oranges	12	2	1
89	Limes (including Lemons and Citron)	12	2	1
90	Pumelows ...	2	2	1
91	Pine Apples	3	2	1
92	Durians ...	2	3	1
93	Plantains (different sorts) ...		2	1
94	Mangosteens	12	2	1
95	Sour Sops ...	3	2	1
96	Custard Apples ...	3	2	1
97	Chikus	2	2	1
98	Collection of Fruit ...		3	1

SECTION VII.—Miscellaneous.

Class.	Kinds.	No. to be exhibited.	Prizes. First.	Second.
			$	$
99	Tapioca Roots...	6	1	
100	Arrowroots	6	1	
101	Ginger Roots	6	1	
102	Turmeric	6	1	
103	Cocoa-nuts (ripe)	6	1	
104	Cacao Fruits	6	1	
105	Nutmegs	12	1	
106	Sugar Cane	...	1	
107	Pepper, sample of fresh	...	1	
108	Arabian Coffee	...	1	
109	Liberian Coffee	...	1	
110	Tea	...	1	
111	Fibre locally prepared from local Plants...		5	
112	Ornamental Flower Stand of local make to hold from 6 to 9 pots		2	1
113	Flower Pots (Earthenware), local make		2	1
114	Flower Tubs (Wood), local make...		2	1
115	Collection of Chinese Plants, in pots, of fantastic shape ...		2	
116	Other vegetable products not included in above		2	

PRIZE LIST

OF THE

FLOWER SHOW

TO BE HELD IN

THE BOTANICAL GARDENS,

ON TWO DAYS TO BE FIXED HEREAFTER

APRIL, 1889.

Open on the 1st Day from 3 p.m. until Dark.
Open on the 2nd Day { From 6 a.m. until 10 a.m.
" 3 p.m. " 6 p.m.
" 8 p.m. " 11 p.m.

ADMISSION.

FIRST DAY... ... $1 EACH PERSON.
SECOND DAY ... { 20 cents before 6 p.m.
{ $1 Evening.

Ticket to admit one person to the whole Exhibition $1.00
Family Tickets do. do. $3.00

Schools and Charitable Institutions will be admitted free on the 2nd Day by the order of an Honorary Secretary, for which application must be made four days previously. Tickets will also be given free for distribution among Market Gardeners.

H. N. RIDLEY,
C. STRINGER,
Honorary Secretaries.

Singapore:
PRINTED AT THE "SINGAPORE AND STRAITS PRINTING OFFICE."

Rules.

1. The competition shall be open to residents in Singapore, Penang, Malacca, and the Native States.

2. All articles exhibited for competition shall have been grown by the exhibitor, or must have been in his possession at least four weeks before the day of exhibition—Bouquets and Table Decorations excepted.

3. It should be distinctly understood that all plants exhibited in Section II. must be in flower, and fruits and vegetables must be fit for use. The plants in all classes which contain more than one kind, must be of dissimilar kinds, except in class 50.

4. All articles included in any entry must be arranged, and the Exhibitors and assistants must finally leave the shed by six p.m. on the day before the Exhibition opens—except Exhibitors in Sections IV., V. and VI., and class 50 who will be allowed to remain until 10 a.m. on the day of opening. Plants in pots cannot be received latter than noon the day before the opening day.

5. The arrangement of the exhibits shall be subject to the directions of the Committee.

6. The Committee will appoint Judges, from whose decision there shall be no appeal.

7. The Judges will have authority to withhold the prize when they are of opinion that there is not sufficient merit to justify an award; or to award special prizes for anything not mentioned in the Schedule.

8. No Exhibitor shall be awarded two prizes in the same class, or more then five prizes in the same Section.

RULES—*Continued.*

9. Intending Exhibitors must give notice to the Honorary Secretary, at least five days before the day of the show, in what classes they intend to exhibit, and must state the space they are likely to require, otherwise their productions may be rejected. On giving this information they will receive numbered cards, which must be attached to the exhibits in place of the Exhibitor's name.

10. No articles included in any entry shall be removed from the shed before the close of the show. Exhibitors will receive a ticket, marked with a number corresponding to that of their exhibits, which must be produced at the close of the show before they can be removed.

If exhibitors will carefully attend to the Rules and Notes, and also label their productions with the numbers of the classes in which they wish them to be shown, confusion and trouble will be avoided.

All reasonable care will be taken of articles while on exhibition

Section I.—Ornamental Foliage Plants in Pots.

Class.	Kinds.	No. to be exhibited.	Prizes.	
			First	Second
			$	$
1	Panax or Aralia	4	1	...
2	Coleus	6	3	2
3	,,	specn.	1	...
4	Crotons	6	3	2
5	,,	specn.	3	...
6	Maranta and Calathea	6	4	2
7	,, ,,	specn.	2	1
8	Palms ...	3	2	...
9	Caladiums	6	3	2
10	,,	specn.	2	...
11	Dieffenbachias	3	2	...
12	Aroids other than the above (Pothos, Scindapsus, Alocasia, Colocasia, Anthurium, &c.) ...	6	3	1
13	,, ,, ,,	specn.	3	...
14	Dracænas	3	2	...
15	Ferns ...	12	10	5
16	,,	6	7	3
17	,,	3	5	2
18	Specimen Fern	...	4	...
19	Tree Fern	specn.	2	...
20	Selaginellas	6	5	2
21	,,	3	3	1
22	Ornamental foliage plants not included in the above	3	2	

Section II.—Plants in Pots, in Flower.

Class.	Kinds.	No. to be exhibited.	Prizes. First.	Second.
			$	$
23	Pansies		2	1
24	Dianthus (Pink)		3	1
25	Camellias		3	1
26	Geraniums		3	1
27	Balsams		2	1
28	Zinnias		4	2
29	Roses		3	1
30	,,	specn.	2	1
31	Asters		3	1
32	Chrysanthemums		3	1
33	Dahlias		2	1
34	Phlox		3	1
35	Petunias		3	1
36	Antirrhinums		2	1
37	Gloxinias		4	2
38	,,	specn.	2	1
39	Other Gesneraceæ (Gesnera, Tydoa, Achimenes, Episcia, &c.)		3	1
40	Verbenas		3	1
41	Gaillardias		3	1
42	Orchids	6	10	4
43	,,	specn.	4	2
44	,,	Rarest	3	...
45	Gladioli		3	1
46	Amaryllids and Lilies		4	2
47	,,		2	...
48	Plant in Flower not included in above	specn.	3	
49	Best collection of different Plants in flower not less than	12	10	0

For all classes in this Section, except classes 42 and 49 and those denoted as specimens, the number of exhibits is not restricted, but in awarding prizes the judges will take into consideration the quantity as well as the quality of each exhibit.

SECTION III.—Plants in Pots, whether in Flower or not.

Class.	Kinds.	No. to be exhibited.	Prizes.	
			First.	Second.
			$	$
50	Group of Plants, arranged for effect in space not exceeding 9 feet square	...	5	3
51	Collection of different Plants..	24	5	3
52	Begonias	12	10	5
53	,,	3	5	2
54	,,	specn.	3	2
55	Cacti	3	2	
56	The rarest Native Plant	...	3	
57	,, Exotic ,,	...	2	...

SECTION IV.—Cut Flowers.

Class.	Kinds.	No. to be exhibited.	Prizes.	
			First. $	Second. $
58	Camellias	speen.	2	1
59	Roses	4	3	1
60	,, ...	2	3	1
61	Asters... ...	3	2	1
62	Chrysanthemums ...	3	3	1
63	Dahlias	3	2	1
64	Collection of Cut Flowers, arranged for effect		5	2
65	Collection of Wild Flowers, arranged for effect ...		5	2
66	Hand Bouquet ...	...	4	1
67	Bridal ,, (White Flowers)		4	1
68	Table decoration		4	1

SECTION V.—Vegetables.

Class.	Kinds.	No. to be exhibited.	Prizes.	
			First.	Second.
			$	$ c.
69	Carrots	6	1	0 50
70	Cucumbers	4	1	0 50
71	Brinjal	4	1	0 50
72	Lettuces	4	1	0 50
73	French Beans	20 pds.	1	0 50
74	Peas	20 ,,	1	0 50
75	Onions or Shallots	12	1	0 50
76	Radishes	12	1	0 50
77	Tomatoes	12	1	0 50
78	Cabbages	2	1	0 50
79	Vegetable Marrows	2	1	0 50
80	Sweet Potato (Kledi)	12	1	
81	,, ,, (Yam)	12	1	
82	Celery	3 stalks.	1	0 50
83	Beet-root	3	1	0 50
84	Artichokes	6	1	0 50
85	Collection of European Vegetables		5	2 00
86	Collection of Native Vegetables		3	1 00

SECTION VI.—Fruits.

Class.	Kinds.	No. to be exhibited.	Prizes.	
			First. $	Second. $
87	Melons	2	2	1
88	Oranges	12	2	1
89	Limes (including Lemons and Citron)	12	2	1
90	Pumelows	2	2	1
91	Pine Apples	3	2	1
92	Durians	2	3	1
93	Plantains (different sorts)		2	1
94	Mangosteens	12	2	1
95	Sour Sops	3	2	1
96	Custard Apples	3	2	1
97	Chikus	2	2	1
98	Collection of Fruit		3	1

SECTION VII.—Miscellaneous.

Class.	Kinds.	No. to be exhibited.	Prizes.	
			First.	Second.
			$	$
99	Tapioca Roots...	6	1	...
100	Arrowroots	6	1	...
101	Ginger Roots ...	6	1	...
102	Turmeric	6	1	...
103	Cocoa-nuts (ripe)	6	1	...
104	Cacao Fruits ...	6	1	...
105	Nutmegs	12	1	...
106	Sugar Cane	...	1	...
107	Pepper, sample of fresh	...	1	...
108	Arabian Coffee	...	1	...
109	Liberian Coffee	...	1	...
110	Tea	...	1	...
111	Fibre locally prepared from local Plants ...	...	5	
112	Ornamental Flower Stand of local make to hold from 6 to 9 pots	...	2	1
113	Flower Pots (Earthenware), local make	...	2	1
114	Flower Tubs (Wood), local make ...	...	2	1
115	Collection of Chinese Plants, in pots, of fantastic shape ...		2	
116	Other vegetable products not included in above ...		2	...

PRIZE LIST

OF THE

FLOWER SHOW

TO BE HELD IN

THE BOTANICAL GARDENS,

ON TUESDAY THE 25TH AND WEDNESDAY THE 26TH MARCH, 1890.

Open on the 1st Day from 3 pm. until Dark.
Open on the 2nd Day { From 6 a.m. until 10 a.m.
,, 3 p.m. ,, 6 p.m.
,, 8 p.m. ,, 11 p.m.

ADMISSION.

FIRST DAY... ... $1 EACH PERSON.
SECOND DAY ... { 20 cents before 6 p.m.
$1 Evening.

Ticket to admit one person to the whole Exhibition $1.50
Family Tickets do. do. $3.00

Schools and Charitable Institutions will be admitted free on the 2nd Day by the order of an Honorary Secretary, for which application must be made four days previously. Tickets will also be given free for distribution among Market Gardeners.

H. N. RIDLEY,
Honorary Secretary.

Singapore:
PRINTED AT THE "SINGAPORE AND STRAITS PRINTING OFFICE."

Rules.

1. The competition shall be open to residents in Singapore, Penang, Malacca, and the Native States.

2. All articles exhibited for competition shall have been grown by the exhibitor, or must have been in his possession at least four weeks before the day of exhibition—Bouquets and Table Decorations excepted.

3. It shall be distinctly understood that all plants exhibited in Section II. must be in flower, and fruits and vegetables must be fit for use. The plants in all classes which contain more than one kind, must be of dissimilar kinds, except in class 50.

4. All articles included in any entry must be arranged, and the Exhibitors and assistants must finally leave the shed by 6 P.M. on the day before the Exhibitions opens—except Exhibitors in Sections IV., V. and VI., and class 50 who will be allowed to remain until 10 A.M. on the day of opening. Plants in pots cannot be received later than noon the day before the opening day.

5. The arrangement of the exhibits shall be subject to the directions of the Committee.

6. The Committee will appoint Judges, from whose decision there shall be no appeal.

7. The Judges will have authority to withhold the prize when they are of opinion that there is not sufficient merit to justify an award; or to award special prizes for anything not mentioned in the Schedule.

8. No Exhibitor shall be awarded two prizes in the same class, or more than five prizes in the same Section.

RULES—*Continued*.

9. Intending Exhibitors must give notice to the Honorary Secretary, at least five days before the day of the show, in what classes they intend to exhibit, and must state the space they are likely to require, otherwise their productions may be rejected. On giving this information they will receive numbered cards, which must be attached to the exhibits in place of the Exhibitor's name.

10. No articles included in any entry shall be removed from the shed before the close of the show. Exhibitors will receive a ticket, marked with a number corresponding to that of their exhibits, which must be produced at the close of the show before they can be removed.

If exhibitors will carefully attend to the Rules and Notes, and also label their productions with the numbers of the classes in which they wish them to be shown, confusion and trouble will be avoided.

All reasonable care will be taken of articles while on exhibition.

Section I.—Ornamental Foliage Plants in Pots.

Class.	Kinds.	No. to be exhibited.	Prizes. First $	Second $
1	Panax or Aralia	4	1	
2	Coleus	6	3	2
3	,,	specn.	1	
4	Crotons	6	3	2
5	,,	specn.	3	
6	Maranta and Calathea.	6	4	2
7	,,	specn.	2	1
8	Palms	3	2	
9	Caladiums	6	3	2
10	,,	specn.	2	
11	Dieffenbachias	3	2	
12	Aroids other than the above (Pothos, Scindapsus, Alocasia, Colocasia, Anthurium, &c.)	6	3	1
13	,, ,,	specn.	3	
14	Dracænas	3	2	
15	Ferns	12	10	5
16	,,	6	7	3
17	,,	3	5	2
18	Specimen Fern		4	
19	Tree Fern	specn.	2	
20	Selaginellas	6	5	2
21	,,	3	3	1
22	Ornamental foliage plants not included in the above	3	2	

Section II.—Plants in Pots, in Flower.

Class.	Kinds.	No. to be exhibited.	Prizes. First.	Second
			$	$
23	Hibiscus	3	3	1
24	,,	specn.	2	1
25	Ixora	3	3	1
26	,,	specn.	2	1
27	Dianthus (Pink)		3	1
28	Camellias		3	1
29	Balsams		3	1
30	Zinnias		2	1
31	Roses		3	1
32	,,	specn.	2	1
33	Asters		3	1
34	Chrysanthemums		3	1
35	Dahlias		3	1
36	Phlox		2	1
37	Petunias		2	1
38	Antirrhinums		2	1
39	Gloxinias		4	2
40	,,	specn.	2	1
41	Other Gesneraceæ (Gesnera, Tydea, Achimenes, Episcia, &c.)		3	1
42	Verbenas		3	1
43	Gaillardias		3	1
44	Orchids	6	10	4
45	,,	specn.	4	2
46	,,	Rarest	3	...
47	Gladioli		3	1
48	Amaryllids and Lilies		4	2
49	,, ,,		2	...
50	Plant in Flower not included in above	specn.	3	
51	Best collection of different Plants in flower not less than	12	10	5

For all classes in this Section, except classes 42 and 49 and those denoted as specimens, the number of exhibits is not restricted, but in awarding prizes the judges will take into consideration the quantity as well as the quality of each exhibit.

SECTION III.—Plants in Pots, whether in Flower or not.

CLASS.	KINDS.	No. to be exhibited.	PRIZES.	
			First.	Second.
			$	$
52	Group of Plants, arranged for effect in space not exceeding 9 feet square ...		5	3
53	Collection of different Plants..	24	10	5
54	Begonias	12	10	5
55	,, ...	3	3	2
56	,, ...	specn.	3	2
57	Succulents	3	2	
58	The rarest Native Plant ...	...	3	
59	,, Exotic	...	2	

SECTION IV.—Cut Flowers.

Class.	Kinds.	No. to be exhibited.	Prizes.	
			First.	Second.
			$	$
60	Camellias	specn.	2	1
61	Roses ...	3	3	1
62	Asters ...	3	2	1
63	Chrysanthemums	3	3	1
64	Dahlias	3	2	1
65	Collection of Cut Flowers, arranged for effect		5	2
66	Collection of Wild Flowers, arranged for effect		5	2
67	Hand Bouquet		4	1
68	Bridal ,, (White Flowers)		4	1
69	Table decoration		4	1

SECTION V.—Vegetables.

Class.	Kinds.	No. to be exhibited.	Prizes.	
			First.	Second.
			$	$ c.
70	Carrots	6	1	0 50
71	Cucumbers	4	1	0 50
72	Brinjal...	4	1	0 50
73	Lettuces	4	1	0 50
74	French Beans ..	20 pds.	1	0 50
75	Peas	20 ,,	1	0 50
76	Onions or Shallots	12	1	0 50
77	Radishes	12	1	0 50
78	Tomatoes	6	1	0 50
79	Cabbages	2	1	0. 50
80	Vegetable Marrows	2	1	0 50
81	Sweet Potato (Kledi)	12	1	
82	,, ,, (Yam)...	12	1	
83	Celery ...	3 stalks	1	0 50
84	Beet-root	3	1	0 50
85	Artichokes	6	1	0 50
86	Chillies	6	1	0 50
87	Collection of European Vegetables	...	5	0 00
88	Collection of Native Vegetables	...	3	1 00

SECTION VI.—Fruits.

Class.	Kinds.	No. to be exhibited.	Prizes. First.	Second.
			$	$
89	Melons	2	2	1
90	Oranges	12	2	1
91	Limes (including Lemons and Citron)	12	2	1
92	Pumelows	2	2	1
93	Pine Apples	3	2	1
94	Durians	2	3	1
95	Plantains (different sorts)	...	2	1
96	Mangosteens	12	2	1
97	Sour Sops	3	2	1
98	Custard Apples	3	2	1
99	Chikus	2	2	1
100	Collection of Fruit	...	3	1

SECTION VII.—Miscellaneous.

Class.	Kinds.	No. to be exhibited.	Prizes. First.	Second.
			$	$
101	Tapioca Roots	6	1	...
102	Arrowroots	6	1	...
103	Ginger Roots	6	1	...
104	Turmeric	6	1	...
105	Cocoa-nuts (ripe)	6	2	...
106	Cacao Fruits	6	2	...
107	Nutmegs	12	2	...
108	Collection of Spices	...	2	...
109	Sugar Cane	...	1	...
110	Pepper, sample of fresh	...	1	...
111	Arabian Coffee	...	2	...
112	Liberian Coffee	...	2	...
113	Tea	...	2	...
114	Fibre locally prepared from local Plants	...	2	...
115	Ornamental Flower Stand of local make, to hold from 6 to 9 pots	...	2	1
116	Flower Pots (Earthenware), local make	...	2	1
117	Flower Tubs (Wood), local make	...	2	1
118	Collection of Chinese Plants, in pots, of fantastic shape	...	2	...
119	Other vegetable products not included in above	...	2	...

PRIZE LIST

OF THE

FLOWER SHOW

TO BE HELD IN

THE BOTANICAL GARDENS,

ON FRIDAY AND SATURDAY,
THE 19TH AND 20TH JUNE, 1891.

Open on the 1st Day from 3 p.m. until Dark.
Open on the 2nd Day { From 6 a.m. until 10 a.m.
                           ,,   3 p.m.   ,,   6 p.m.
                           ,,   8 p.m.   ,,   11 p.m.

ADMISSION.

FIRST DAY... $1 EACH PERSON.
SECOND DAY   { 20 cents before 6 p.m.
                           { $1 Evening.

Ticket to admit one person to the whole Exhibition $1.50
Family Tickets   do.   do. $3.00

     Schools and Charitable Institutions will be admitted free on the 2nd Day by the order of an Honorary Secretary, for which application must be made four days previously. Tickets will also be given free for distribution among Market Gardeners.

H. N. RIDLEY,
Honorary Secretary.

Singapore:
PRINTED AT THE "SINGAPORE AND STRAITS PRINTING OFFICE."

COMMITTEE.

Hon. MAJOR MCCALLUM, R.E., C.M.G.

His Honor MR. JUSTICE GOLDNEY.

R. W. HULLETT, Esq.

JAMES MILLER, Esq.

C. STRINGER, Esq.

J. B. SAUNDERS, Esq.

Colonel BURTON BROWN.

SEAH LIANG SEAH.

SEAH SONG SEAH.

W. NANSON, Esq.

CHOA KIM KEAT, Esq.

DATOH DALAM.

D. G. PRESGRAVE, Esq.

ST. VINCENT B. DOWN, Esq.

H. C. JOHNSTON, Esq.

H. N. RIDLEY,
Hon. Secretary.

Rules.

1. The competition shall be open to residents in Singapore, Penang, Malacca, and the Native States.

2. All articles exhibited for competition shall have been grown by the exhibitor, or must have been in his possession at least four weeks before the day of exhibition—Bouquets and Table Decorations excepted.

3. It shall be distinctly understood that all plants exhibited in Section II. must be in flower, and fruits and vegetables must be fit for use. The plants in all classes which contain more than one kind, must be of dissimilar kinds, except in class 50.

4. All articles included in any entry must be arranged, and the Exhibitors and assistants must finally leave the shed by 6 P.M. on the day before the Exhibition opens—except Exhibitors in Sections IV., V. and VI., who will be allowed to remain until 10 A.M. on the day of opening. Plants in pots cannot be received later than noon the day before the opening day.

5. The arrangement of the exhibits shall be subject to the directions of the Committee.

6. The Committee will appoint Judges, from whose decision there shall be no appeal.

7. The Judges will have authority to withhold the prize when they are of opinion that there is not sufficient merit to justify an award; or to award special prizes for anything not mentioned in the Schedule.

8. No Exhibitor shall be awarded two prizes in the same class, or more than five prizes in the same Section.

RULES—Continued.

9. Intending Exhibitors must give notice to the Honorary Secretary, at least five days before the day of the show, in what classes they intend to exhibit, and must state the space they are likely to require, otherwise their productions may be rejected. On giving this information they will receive numbered cards, which must be attached to the exhibits in place of the Exhibitor's name.

10. No articles included in any entry shall be removed from the shed before the close of the show. Exhibitors will receive a ticket, marked with a number corresponding to that of their exhibits, which must be produced at the close of the show before they can be removed.

If exhibitors will carefully attend to the Rules and Notes, and also label their productions with the numbers of the classes in which they wish them to be shown, confusion and trouble will be avoided.

All reasonable care will be taken of articles while on exhibition.

Section I.—Ornamental Foliage Plants in Pots.

Class.	Kinds.	No. to be exhibited.	Prizes.	
			First $	Second $
1	Panax or Aralia	4	1	...
2	Coleus	6	3	2
3	,,	specn.	1	...
4	Crotons	6	3	2
5	,,	specn.	3	...
6	Maranta and Calathea	6	4	2
7	,, ,, ,,	specn.	2	1
8	Palms	3	2	...
9	Palm	specn.	1	...
10	Caladiums	6	3	2
11	,,	3	2	1
12	,,	specn.	2	...
13	Dieffenbachias	3	2	...
14	Aroids other than the above (Pothos, Scindapsus, Alocasia, Colocasia, Anthurium, &c.)	6	3	1
15	,, ,,	specn.	3	...
16	Dracænas	3	2	...
17	Ferns	12	10	5
18	,,	6	7	3
19	,,	3	5	2
20	Specimen Fern	...	4	...
21	Tree Fern	specn.	2	...
22	Selaginellas	6	5	2
23	,,	3	3	1
24	,,	specn.	2	...
25	Ornamental foliage plants not included in the above	3	2	...

Section II.—Plants in Pots, in Flower.

CLASS.	KINDS.	No. to be exhibited.	PRIZES. First.	Second
			$	$
26	Hibiscus	3	3	1
27	,,	specn.	2	1
28	Ixora	3	3	1
29	,,	specn.	2	1
30	Dianthus (Pink)		3	1
31	Camellias		3	1
32	Balsams		3	1
33	Zinnias		2	1
34	Roses		3	1
35	,,	specn.	2	1
36	Asters		3	1
37	Chrysanthemums		3	1
38	Dahlias		3	1
39	Phlox		2	1
40	Petunias		2	1
41	Antirrhinums (Snapdragon)		2	1
42	Gloxinias		4	2
43	,,	specn.	2	1
44	Other Gesneraceæ (Gesnera, Tydea, Achimenes, Episcia, &c.)		3	1
45	Verbenas		3	1
46	Gaillardias		3	1
47	Orchids	6	10	4
48	,,	specn.	4	2
49	,,	rarest	3	
50	Gladioli		3	1
51	Amaryllids and Lilies		4	2
52	,, ,, ,,	specn.	2	
53	Plant in Flower not included in above	specn.	3	
54	Best collection of different Plants in flower not less than	12	10	5

For all classes in this Section, except classes 26, 28, 47 and 54 and those denoted as specimens, the number of exhibits is not restricted, but in awarding prizes the judges will take into consideration the quantity as well as the quality of each exhibit.

SECTION III.—Plants in Pots, whether in Flower or not.

Class.	Kinds.	No to be exhibited.	Prizes. First. $	Second. $
55	Group of Plants, arranged for effect in space not exceeding 9 feet square ...		5	3
56	Collection of different Plants..	24	5	3
57	Begonias ...	12	10	5
58	,, ...	3	3	2
59	,, ...	specn.	3	2
60	Succulents ...	3	2	
61	The rarest Native Plant ...	...	3	...
62	,, Exotic ...		2	

SECTION IV.—Cut Flowers.

Class.	Kinds.	No. to be exhibited.	Prizes. First.	Second.
			$	$
63	Camellias ...	specn.	2	1
64	Roses Not less than	3	3	1
65	Asters ... ,,	3	2	1
66	Chrysanthemums ,,	3	3	1
67	Dahlias ... ,,	3	2	1
68	Buttonholes and Sprays ,,	4	3	1
69	Collection of Cut Flowers, arranged for effect		5	2
70	Collection of Wild Flowers, arranged for effect... ...		5	2
71	Hand Bouquet	...	4	1
72	Bridal ,, (White Flowers)	...	4	1
73	Table decoration	...	4	1

SECTION V.—Vegetables.

CLASS.	KINDS.	No. to be exhibited.	PRIZES. First.	Second.
			$	$ c.
74	Carrots	6	1	0 50
75	Cucumbers	4	1	0 50
76	Brinjal	4	1	0 50
77	Lettuces	4	1	0 50
78	French Beans	20 pds.	1	0 50
79	Peas	20 ,,	1	0 50
80	Onions or Shallots	12	1	0 50
81	Radishes	12	1	0 50
82	Tomatoes	6	1	0 50
83	Cabbages	2	1	0 50
84	Vegetable Marrows	2	1	0 50
85	Sweet Potato (Kledi)	12	1	
86	,, (Yam)	12	1	
87	Celery	3 stalks	1	0 50
88	Beet-root	3	1	0 50
89	Artichokes	6	1	0 50
90	Chillies	6	1	0 50
91	Collection of European Vegetables		5	
92	Collection of Native Vegetables		3	1 00
93	Any Vegetable not included in the above	...	1	0 50

SECTION VI.—Fruits.

Class.	Kinds.	No. to be exhibited.	Prizes.	
			First.	Second.
			$	$
94	Melons	2	2	1
95	Oranges	12	2	1
96	Limes (including Lemons and Citron)	12	2	1
97	Pumelows	2	2	1
98	Pine Apples	3	2	1
99	Durians	2	3	1
100	Plantains (different sorts)		2	1
101	Mangosteens	12	2	1
102	Sour Sops	3	2	1
103	Custard Apples	3	2	1
104	Chikus	2	2	1
105	Collection of Fruit		3	1

SECTION VII.—Miscellaneous.

Class.	Kinds.	No. to be ex-hibited.	Prizes.	
			First. $	Second. $
106	Tapioca Roots	6	1	...
107	Arrowroots	6	1	
108	Ginger Roots	6	1	
109	Turmeric	6	1	
110	Cocoa-nuts (ripe)	6	2	...
111	Cacao Fruits	6	2	...
112	Nutmegs	12	2	...
113	Collection of Spices		2	...
114	Sugar Cane	...	1	
115	Pepper, sample of fresh	...	1	
116	Arabian Coffee		2	
117	Liberian Coffee	...	2	...
118	Tea	...	2	...
119	Fibre locally prepared from local Plants...		2	
120	Collection of Chinese Plants, in pots, of fantastic shape...	...	2	1
121	Other vegetable products not included in above ...	...	2	

PRIZE LIST

OF THE

Flower Show

TO BE HELD IN THE

TOWN HALL,

ON

SATURDAY, the 26th AUGUST, 1893.

Open from 4 p.m. to 7 p.m. and from 8 p.m. to 11 p.m.

ADMISSION.

Each Person { From 4 p.m. till 7 p.m.   **50 cts.**
                „   8 „   „ 11 „   ... **50 cts.**
Family Tickets   **$2.**

H. N. RIDLEY,
Honorary Secretary.

Singapore:
Printed at "The Singapore and Straits Printing Office."

COMMITTEE.

H. E. MAJOR-GENERAL SIR CHARLES WARREN, G.C.M.G., K.C.B.

The Hon. SIR E. C. BOVILL

Hon. MAJOR McCALLUM, R.E., C.M.G.

Hon. G. S. MURRAY

R. W. HULLETT, Esq.

W. NANSON, Esq.

SEAH LIANG SEAH

DATOH DALAM

C. W. S. KYNNERSLEY, Esq.

R. H. PADDAY, Esq.

J. P. JOAQUIM, Esq.

ST. VINCENT B. DOWN, Esq.

R. LITTLE, Esq.

H. N. RIDLEY,
Hon. Secretary.

Rules.

1. The competition shall be open to residents in Singapore, Penang, Malacca, and the Native States.

2. All articles exhibited for competition shall have been grown by the exhibitor, or must have been in his possession at least four weeks before the day of Exhibition—Bouquets and Table Decorations excepted.

3. It shall be distinctly understood that all plants exhibited in Section II. must be in flower, and fruits and vegetables must be fit for use.

4. All articles included in any entry must be arranged, and the exhibitors and assistants must finally leave the Hall, by noon on the day of the Exhibition.

5. The arrangement of the exhibits shall be subject to the directions of the Committee.

6. The Committee will appoint Judges, from whose decision there shall be no appeal.

7. The Judges will have authority to withhold the prize when they are of opinion that there is not sufficient merit to justify an award; or to award special prizes for anything not mentioned in the Schedule.

8. No Exhibitor shall be awarded two prizes in the same class, or more than five prizes in the same Section.

9. Intending Exhibitors are requested to give notice to the Honorary Secretary, at least five days before the day of the show, in what classes they intend to exhibit. On giving this

information they will receive numbered cards, which must be attached to the exhibits in place of the exhibitor's name.

10. No articles included in any entry shall be removed from the Hall before the close of the Show. Exhibitors will receive a ticket, marked with a number corresponding to that of their exhibits, which must be produced at the close of the Show before they can be removed.

If exhibitors will carefully attend to the Rules and Notes, and also label their productions with the numbers of the classes in which they wish them to be shown, confusion and trouble will be avoided.

All reasonable care will be taken of articles while on exhibition, but it must be distinctly understood that under no circumstances are the Committee liable for any damage that may occur.

SECTION I.—Ornamental Foliage Plants in Pots.

Class.	Kinds.	No. to be exhibited.	Prizes. First. $	Second. $
1	Panax or Aralia	3	1	...
2	Coleus ...	4	3	2
3	,,	specn.	1	...
4	Crotons	4	3	2
5	,,	specn.	3	...
6	Maranta and Calathea	4	4	2
7	,, ,, ,,	specn.	2	1
8	Palms ...	3	2	...
9	Palm ...	specn.	1	...
10	Caladiums	6	3	2
11	,,	3	2	1
12	,,	specn.	2	...
13	Dieffenbachias	3	2	...
14	Aroids other than the above (Pothos, Scindapsus, Alocasia, Colocasia, Anthurium, &c.) ...	3	3	1
15	,, ,, ,,	specn.	3	...
16	Dracænas	3	2	...
17	Ferns ...	12	10	5
18	,,	6	7	3
19	,,	3	5	2
20	Specimen Fern	...	4	...
21	Tree Fern	specn.	2	...
22	Selaginellas	3	3	1
23	,,	specn.	2	...
24	Ornamental foliage plants not included in the above	3	2	

SECTION II.—Plants in Pots, in Flower.

Class.	Kinds.	No. to be exhibited.	Prizes. First.	Second
			$	$
25	Hibiscus	3	3	1
26	,,	specn.	2	1
27	Ixora	3	3	1
28	,,	specn.	2	1
29	Cockscombs	3	2	1
30	Dianthus (Pink)		3	1
31	Camellias		3	1
32	Balsams		3	1
33	Zinnias		2	1
34	Roses		3	1
35	,,	specn.	2	1
36	Asters		3	1
37	Chrysanthemums		3	1
38	Dahlias		3	1
39	Phlox		2	1
40	Petunias		2	1
41	Antirrhinums (Snapdragon)		2	1
42	Gloxinias		4	2
43	,,	specn.	2	1
44	Other Gesneraceæ (Gesnera, Tydea, Achimenes, Episcia, &c.)		3	1
45	Verbenas		3	1
46	Gaillardias		3	1
47	Orchids	6	10	4
48	,,	specn.	4	2
49	,, *	rarest	3	...
50	Gladioli		3	1
51	Amaryllids and Lilies		4	2
52	,, ,, ,,	specn.	2	...
53	Plant in Flower not included in above	specn.	3	
54	Best collection of different Plants in flower not less than	12	10	5

For all classes in this Section, except classes 26, 38, 47 and 54 and those denoted as specimens, the number of exhibits is not restricted, but in awarding prizes the judges will take into consideration the quantity as well as the quality of each exhibit.

* Special prize for Rarest Orchid in show.

SECTION III.—Plants in Pots, whether in Flower or not.

Class.	Kinds.	No. to be exhibited.	Prizes.	
			First. $	Second $
55	Begonias	6	5	3
56	,,	3	3	2
57	,,	specn.	3	2
58	Succulents	3	2	
59	The rarest Native Plant		3	
60	,, Exotic		2	

SECTION IV.—Cut Flowers.

Class.	Kinds.	No. to be exhibited.	Prizes.	
			First. $	Second $
61	Camellias	specn.	2	1
62	Roses Not less than	3	3	1
63	Asters... ,,	3	2	1
64	Chrysanthemums ,,	3	3	1
65	Dahlias ,,	3	2	1
66	Gardenias	3	3	1
67	Ixoras ...	3	3	1
68	Stephanotis	3	2	1
69	Sunflowers	3	2	1
70	Buttonholes and Sprays ,,	4	3	1
71	Collection of Cut Flowers, arranged for effect		5	1
72	Cut Flowers Specimens	6	3	1
73	Collection of Wild Flowers, arranged for effect		5	2
74	Hand Bouquet		4	1
75	Bridal ,, (White Flowers)		4	1
76	* Table Decoration		4	1

* The size of the tables will be 10 feet by 4.

SECTION V.—Vegetables.

Class.	Kinds.	No. to be exhibited.	Prizes.	
			First.	Second
			$	$ c.
77	Carrots	6	1	0 50
78	Cucumbers	4	1	0 50
79	Brinjal...	4	1	0 50
80	Lettuces	4	1	0 50
81	French Beans ...	20 pds.	1	0 50
82	Peas	20 ,,	1	0 50
83	Onions or Shallots	12	1	0 50
84	Radishes	12	1	0 50
85	Tomatoes	6	1	0 50
86	Cabbages	2	1	0 50
87	Vegetable Marrows	2	1	0 50
88	Sweet Potato (Kledi)	12	1	
89	,, ,, (Yam)	12	1	
90	Celery ...	3 stalks	1	0 50
91	Beet-root	3	1	0 50
92	Artichokes	6	1	0 50
93	Chillies	6	1	0 50
94	Collection of European Vegetables	...	5	...
95	Collection of Native Vegetables		3	1 00
96	Any Vegetable not included in the above	...	1	0 50

SECTION VI.—Fruits.

Class.	Kinds.	No. to be exhibited.	Prizes.	
			First. $	Second. $
97	Melons...	2	2	1
98	Oranges ...	12	2	1
99	Limes (including Lemons and Citron)	12	2	1
100	Pumelows	2	2	1
101	Pine Apples	3	2	1
102	Durians ...	2	3	1
103	Plantains (different sorts) ...		2	1
104	Mangosteens	12	2	1
105	Sour Sops	3	2	1
106	Custard Apples ...	3	2	1
107	Chikus... ...	2	2	1
108	Collection of Fruit		3	1

SECTION VII.—Miscellaneous.

Class.	Kinds.	No. to be exhibited.	Prizes.	
			First. $	Second $
109	Tapioca Roots	6	1	...
110	Arrowroots	6	1	
111	Ginger Roots	6	1	...
112	Turmeric	6	1	
113	Cocoa-nuts (ripe)	6	2	
114	Cacao Fruits	6	2	
115	Nutmegs	12	2	
116	Collection of Spices		2	
117	Sugar Cane		1	
118	Pepper, sample of fresh		1	
119	Arabian Coffee		2	
120	Liberian Coffee		2	
121	Tea		2	
122	Collection of Chinese Plants, in pots, of fantastic shape		2	1
123	Other vegetable products not included in above		2	

PRIZE LIST

OF THE

Flower Show

TO BE HELD IN THE

S. V. A. DRILL HALL,

ON

Thursday and Friday the 14th and 15th June, 1894.

FIRST DAY.

Open from 4 p.m. to 7 p.m.

Admission, each person $1

SECOND DAY.

Open from 10 a.m. to 6 p.m.   50 cts.

and from 8 p.m. to 11 p.m. $1 ...

H. N. RIDLEY,
Honorary Secretary.

Singapore:

PRINTED AT "THE SINGAPORE AND STRAITS PRINTING OFFICE."

COMMITTEE.

R. W. HULLETT, Esq.
W. NANSON, Esq.
C. STRINGER, Esq.
R. LITTLE, Esq.
ST. V. B. DOWN, Esq.
J. P. JOAQUIM, Esq.

E. J. KHORY, Esq.
R. H. PADDAY, Esq.
LEE CHEANG YEAN, Esq.
SEE EWE LAY, Esq.
LIANG SEAH, Esq.
CHOA KIM KEAT, Esq.

H. N. RIDLEY,
Hon. Secretary.

Rules.

1. The competition shall be open to residents in Singapore, Penang, Malacca, and the Native States.

2. All articles exhibited for competition shall have been grown by the exhibitor, or must have been in his possession at least four weeks before the day of Exhibition—Bouquets and Table Decorations excepted.

3. It shall be distinctly understood that all plants exhibited in Section II. must be in flower, and fruits and vegetables must be fit for use.

4. All articles included in any entry must be arranged, and the exhibitors and assistants must finally leave the Hall, by noon on the day of the Exhibition.

5. The arrangement of the exhibits shall be subject to the directions of the Committee.

6. The Committee will appoint Judges, from whose decision there shall be no appeal.

7. The Judges will have authority to withhold the prize when they are of opinion that there is not sufficient merit to justify an award; or to award special prizes for anything not mentioned in the Schedule.

8. No Exhibitor shall be awarded two prizes in the same class, or more than five prizes in the same Section.

9. Intending Exhibitors are requested to give notice to the Honorary Secretary, at least five days before the day of the show, in what classes they intend to exhibit. On giving this

information they will receive numbered cards, which must be attached to the exhibits in place of the exhibitor's name.

10. No articles included in any entry shall be removed from the Hall before the close of the Show. Exhibitors will receive a ticket, marked with a number corresponding to that of their exhibits, which must be produced at the close of the Show before they can be removed.

If exhibitors will carefully attend to the Rules and Notes, and also label their productions with the numbers of the classes in which they wish them to be shown, confusion and trouble will be avoided.

All reasonable care will be taken of articles while on exhibition, but it must be distinctly understood that under no circumstances are the Committee liable for any damage that may occur.

SECTION I.—Ornamental Foliage Plants in Pots.

Class.	Kinds.	No. to be exhibited.	Prizes.	
			First.	Second
			$	$
1	Panax or Aralia	3	1	...
2	Coleus	4	3	2
3	,,	specn.	1	...
4	Crotons	4	3	2
5	,,	specn.	3	...
6	Maranta and Calathea	4	4	2
7	,, ,,	specn.	2	1
8	Palms	3	2	...
9	Palm	specn.	1	...
10	Caladiums	6	3	2
11	,,	3	2	1
12	,,	specn.	2	...
13	Dieffenbachias	3	2	...
14	Aroids other than the above (Pothos, Scindapsus, Alocasia, Colocasia, Anthurium, &c.)	3	3	1
15	,,	specn.	3	...
16	Dracænas	3	2	...
17	Ferns	12	7	3
18	,,	6	5	2
19	,,	3	5	2
20	Specimen Fern	...	4	...
21	Tree Fern	specn.	2	...
22	Selaginellas	3	3	1
23	,,	specn.	2	...
24	Ornamental foliage plants not included in the above	3	2	

SECTION II.—Plants in Pots, in Flower.

Class.	Kinds.	No. to be exhibited.	Prizes.	
			First.	Second
			$	$
25	Hibiscus	3	3	1
26	,,	specn.	2	1
27	Ixora	3	3	1
28	,,	specn.	2	1
29	Cockscombs		2	1
30	Dianthus (Pink)		3	1
31	Camellias		3	1
32	Balsams		3	1
33	Zinnias		2	1
34	Roses		3	1
35	,,	specn.	2	1
36	Asters		3	1
37	Chrysanthemums		3	1
38	Dahlias		3	1
39	Phlox		2	1
40	Petunias		2	1
41	Antirrhinums (Snapdragon)		2	1
42	Gloxinias		4	2
43	,,	specn,	2	1
44	Other Gesneraceæ (Gesnera, Tydea, Achimenes, Episcia, &c.)		3	1
45	Verbenas		3	1
46	Gaillardias		3	1
47	Orchids	6	10	4
48	,,	specn.	4	2
49	Gladioli		3	1
50	Amaryllids and Lilies		4	2
51	,, ,, ,,	specn.	2	...
52	Plant in flower not included in above	specu.	3	
53	Best collection of different Plants in flower not less than	12	10	5

For all classes in this Section, except classes 26, 28, 47 and 54 and those denoted as specimens, the number of exhibits is not restricted, but in awarding prizes the judges will take into consideration the quantity as well as the quality of each exhibit
* Special prize for Rarest Orchid in show, $3.

SECTION III.—Plants in Pots, whether in Flower or not.

Class.	Kinds.	No. to be exhibited.	Prizes.	
			First.	Second
			$	$
54	Begonias	12	5	3
55	,,	6	5	3
56	,,	3	3	2
57	,,	specn.	3	2
58	Succulents	3	2	
59	The rarest Native Plant		3	
60	,, Exotic		2	

SECTION IV.—Cut Flowers.

Class.	Kinds.	No. to be exhibited.	Prizes. First.	Second
			$	$
61	Camellias	specn.	2	1
62	Roses Not less than	3	3	1
63	Asters ... ,,	3	2	1
64	Chrysanthemums ,,	3	3	1
65	Dahlias ,,	3	2	1
66	Gardenias ...	3	3	1
67	Ixoras ...	3	3	1
68	Stephanotis ...	3	2	1
69	Sunflowers ...	3	2	1
70	Buttonholes and Sprays ,,	4	3	1
71	Collection of Cut Flowers, arranged for effect		5	1
72	Cut Flowers Specimens ...	6	3	1
73	Collection of Wild Flowers, arranged for effect		5	2
74	Hand Bouquet ...		4	1
75	Bridal (White Flowers)		4	1
76	* Table Decoration ...		4	1

* The size of the tables will be 10 feet by 4.

SECTION V.—Vegetables.

Class.	Kinds.	No. to be exhibited.	Prizes.	
			First.	Second
			$	$ c.
77	Carrots...	6	1	0 50
78	Cucumbers	4	1	0 50
79	Brinjal...	4	1	0 50
80	Lettuces	4	1	0 50
81	French Beans ...	20 pds.	1	0 50
82	Peas	20 ,,	1	0 50
83	Onions or Shallots	12	1	0 50
84	Radishes	12	1	0 50
85	Tomatoes	6	1	0 50
86	Cabbages	2	1	0 50
87	Vegetable Marrows	2	1	0 50
88	Sweet Potato (Kledi)	12	1	
89	., (Yam) ...	12	1	
90	Celery	3 stalks	1	0 50
91	Beet-root	3	1	0 50
92	Artichokes	6	1	0 50
93	Chillies...	6	1	0 50
94	Collection of European Vegetables	} ...	5	...
95	Collection of Native Vegetables		3	1 00
96	Any Vegetable not included in the above	} ...	1	0 50

SECTION VI.—Fruits.

Class.	Kinds.	No. to be exhibited.	Prizes. First. $	Second. $
97	Melons ...	2	2	1
98	Oranges	12	2	1
99	Limes (including Lemons and Citron)	12	2	1
100	Pumelows	2	2	1
101	Pine Apples	3	2	1
102	Durians	2	3	1
103	Plantains (different sorts)		2	1
104	Mangosteens	12	2	1
105	Sour Sops	3	2	1
106	Custard Apples	3	2	1
107	Chikus ...	2	2	1
108	Collection of Fruit		3	1

SECTION VII.—Miscellaneous.

Class.	Kinds.	No. to be exhibited.	Prizes.	
			First.	Second
			$	$
109	Tapioca Roots	6	1	...
110	Arrowroots	6	1	
111	Ginger Roots ...	6	1	
112	Turmeric	6	1	
113	Cocoa-nuts (ripe)	6	2	
114	Cacao Fruits ...	6	2	
115	Nutmegs	12	2	
116	Collection of Spices ...		2	
117	Sugar Cane	...	1	
118	Pepper, sample of fresh		1	
119	Arabian Coffee		2	...
120	Liberian Coffee		2	
121	Tea		2	
122	Collection of Chinese Plants, in pots, of fantastic shape...		2	1
123	Other vegetable products not included in above ...		2	

PRIZE LIST

OF THE

Flower Show

TO BE HELD IN THE

S. V. A. DRILL HALL,

ON

Friday and Saturday the 5th and 6th July, 1895.

FIRST DAY.

Open from 4 p.m. to 7 p.m.

Admission, each person $1

SECOND DAY.

Open from 10 a.m. to 6 p.m.   **50 cts.**

and from 8 p.m. to 11 p.m.   **$1** ...

W. FOX,

Honorary Secretary.

Singapore:

PRINTED AT "THE SINGAPORE AND STRAITS PRINTING OFFICE."

COMMITTEE.

Hon. J. K. Birch.
R. W. Hullett, Esq.
W. Nanson, Esq.
C. Stringer, Esq.
R. Little, Esq.
H. Eschke, Esq.

J. P. Joaquim, Esq.
J. R. Hilty, Esq.
The Datoh Dalam.
E. J. Khory, Esq.
R. H. Padday, Esq.
Choa Kim Keat, Esq.

W. FOX,
Honorary Secretary.

Rules.

1. The competition shall be open to residents in Singapore, Penang, Malacca, and the Native States.

2. All articles exhibited for competition shall have been grown by the exhibitor, or must have been in his possession at least four weeks before the day of Exhibition—Bouquets and Table Decorations excepted.

3. It shall be distinctly understood that all plants exhibited in Section II. must be in flower, and fruits and vegetables must be fit for use.

4. All articles included in any entry must be arranged, and the exhibitors and assistants must finally leave the Hall, by noon on the day of the Exhibition.

5. The arrangement of the exhibits shall be subject to the directions of the Committee.

6. The Committee will appoint Judges, from whose decision there shall be no appeal.

7. The Judges will have authority to withhold the prize when they are of opinion that there is not sufficient merit to justify an award; or to award special prizes for anything not mentioned in the Schedule.

8. No Exhibitor shall be awarded two prizes in the same class, or more than five prizes in the same Section.

9. Intending Exhibitors are requested to give notice to the Honorary Secretary, at least five days before the day of the show, in what classes they intend to exhibit. On giving this

information they will receive numbered cards, which must be attached to the exhibits in place of the exhibitor's name.

10. No articles included in any entry shall be removed from the Hall before the close of the Show. Exhibitors will receive a ticket, marked with a number corresponding to that of their exhibits, which must be produced at the close of the Show before they can be removed.

If exhibitors will carefully attend to the Rules and Notes, and also label their productions with the numbers of the classes in which they wish them to be shown, confusion and trouble will be avoided.

All reasonable care will be taken of articles while on exhibition, but it must be distinctly understood that under no circumstances are the Committee liable for any damage that may occur.

SECTION I.—Ornamental Foliage Plants in Pots.

Class.	Kinds.	No. to be exhibited.	Prizes.	
			First.	Second
			$	$
1	Panax or Aralia	3	1	...
2	Coleus	4	3	2
3	,,	specn.	1	...
4	Crotons	4	3	2
5	,,	specn.	3	...
6	Maranta and Calathea	4	4	2
7	,, ,, ,,	specn.	2	1
8	Palms	3	2	...
9	Palm	specn.	1	...
10	Caladiums	6	3	2
11	,,	3	2	1
12	,,	specn.	2	...
13	Dieffenbachias	3	2	...
14	Aroids other than the above (Pothos, Scindapsus, Alocasia, Colocasia, Anthurium, &c.)	3	3	1
15	,, ,, ,,	specn.	3	...
16	Dracænas	3	2	...
17	Ferns	12	7	3
18	,,	6	5	2
19	,,	3	5	2
20	Specimen Fern	...	4	...
21	Tree Fern	specn.	2	...
22	Selaginellas	3	3	1
23	,,	specn.	2	...
24	Ornamental foliage plants not included in the above	3	2	

SECTION II.—Plants in Pots, in Flower.

Class.	Kinds.	No. to be exhibited.	Prizes. First	Second
			$	$
25	Hibiscus	3	3	1
26	,,	specn.	2	1
27	Ixora	3	3	1
28	,,	specn.	2	1
29	Cockscombs		2	1
30	Dianthus (Pink)		3	1
31	Camellias		3	1
32	Balsams		3	1
33	Zinnias		2	1
34	Roses		3	1
35	,,	specn.	2	1
36	Asters		3	1
37	Chrysanthemums		3	1
38	Dahlias		3	1
39	Phlox		2	1
40	Petunias		2	1
41	Antirrhinums (Snapdragon)		2	1
42	Gloxinias		4	2
43	,,	specn.	2	1
44	Other Gesneraceæ (Gesnera, Tydea, Achimenes, Episcia, &c.)		3	1
45	Verbenas		3	1
46	Gaillardias		3	1
47	Orchids	6	10	4
48	,,	specn.	4	2
49	Gladioli		3	1
50	Amaryllids and Lilies		4	2
51	,, ,, ,,	specn.	2	...
52	Plant in flower not included in above	specn.	3	
53	Best collection of different Plants in flower, not less than	12	10	5

For all classes in this Section, except classes 36, 28 and 47 and those denoted as specimens, the number of exhibits is not restricted, but in awarding prizes the judges will take into consideration the quantity as well as the quality of each exhibit.

* Special prize for Rarest Orchid in show, $3.

SECTION III.—Plants in Pots, whether in Flower or not.

Class.	Kinds.	No. to be exhibited.	Prizes.	
			First.	Second
			$	$
54	Begonias	12	5	3
55	,,	6	5	3
56	,,	3	3	2
57	,,	specn.	3	2
58	Succulents	3	2	
59	The rarest Native Plant	...	3	
60	,, Exotic	...	2	

SECTION IV.—Cut Flowers.

Class.	Kinds.	No. to be exhibited.	Prizes. First. $	Second. $
61	Camellias ...	specn.	2	1
62	Roses Not less than	3	3	1
63	Asters ... ,,	.3	2	1
64	Chrysanthemums ,,	3	3	1
65	Dahlias... ,,	3	2	1
66	Gardenias ...	3	3	1
67	Ixoras	3	3	1
68	Stephanotis ...	3	2	1
69	Sunflowers	3	2	1
70	Buttonholes and Sprays ,, ...	4	3	1
71	Collection of Cut Flowers, arranged for effect		5	1
72	Cut Flowers, Specimens ...	6	3	1
73	Collection of Wild Flowers, arranged for effect	...	5	2
74	Hand Bouquet	...	4	1
75	Bridal ,, (White Flowers)	...	4	1
76	* Table Decoration ...		4	1

* The size of the Tables will be 10 feet by ¼.

SECTION V.—Vegetables.

Class.	Kinds.	No. to be exhibited.	Prizes. First.	Second
			$	$ c.
77	Carrots...	6	1	0 50
78	Cucumbers	4	1	0 50
79	Brinjal...	4	1	0 50
80	Lettuces	4	1	0 50
81	French Beans...	20 pds.	1	0 50
82	Peas	20 pds.	1	0 50
83	Onions or Shallots	12	1	0 50
84	Radishes	12	1	0 50
85	Tomatoes	6	1	0 50
86	Cabbages	2	1	0 50
87	Vegetable Marrows	2	1	0 50
88	Sweet Potato (Kledi)	12	1	
89	,, ,, (Yam)...	12	1	
90	Celery...	3 stalks	1	0 50
91	Beet-root	3	1	0 50
92	Artichokes	6	1	0 50
93	Chillies...	6	1	0 50
94	Collection of European Vegetables		5	...
95	Collection of Native Vegetables		3	1 00
96	Any Vegetable not included in the above	...	1	0 50

SECTION VI.—Fruits.

Class.	Kinds.	No. to be exhibited.	Prizes.	
			First. $	Second $
97	Melons ...	2	2	1
98	Oranges	12	2	1
99	Limes (including Lemons and Citron)	12	2	1
100	Pumelows	2	2	1
101	Pine Apples	3	2	1
102	Durians	2	3	1
103	Plantains (different sorts) ...		2	1
104	Mangosteens ...	12	2	1
105	Sour Sops	3	2	1
106	Custard Apples	3	2	1
107	Chikus ...	2	2	1
108	Collection of Fruit	...	3	1

SECTION VII.—Miscellaneous.

Class.	Kinds.	No. to be exhibited.	Prizes.	
			First. $	Second $
109	Tapioca Roots	6	1	...
110	Arrowroots	6	1	...
111	Ginger Roots	6	1	
112	Turmeric	6	1	
113	Cocoa-nuts (ripe)	6	2	
114	Cacao Fruits	6	2	...
115	Nutmegs	12	2	
116	Collection of Spices		2	
117	Sugar Cane	...	1	...
118	Pepper, sample of fresh		1	...
119	Arabian Coffee		2	
120	Liberian Coffee		2	
121	Tea		2	
122	Collection of Chinese Plants, in pots, of fantastic shape	...	2	1
123	Other vegetable products not included in above		2	

PRIZE LIST

OF THE

Flower Show

TO BE HELD IN THE

TOWN HALL,

ON

Thursday and Friday the 13th & 14th May, 1897.

FIRST DAY.

Open from 4 p.m. to 7 p.m

Admission, each person - - - $1

SECOND DAY.

Open from 10 a.m. to 6 p.m. .   50 cts.

and from 8 p.m. to 11 p.m. - $1

H. N. RIDLEY,

Honorary Secretary.

Singapore:

Printed at "The Singapore and Straits Printing Office."

COMMITTEE.

ST. V. B. DOWN, Esq.
R. W. HULLETT, Esq.
R. LITTLE, Esq.
J. R. CUTHBERTSON, Esq.
A. P. ADAMS, Esq.
E. E. H. BRYDGES, Esq.
COL. PENNEFATHER.

W. H. SHELFORD, Esq.
J. P. JOAQUIM, Esq.
THE DATOH DALAM.
E. J. KHORY, Esq.
R. H. PADDAY, Esq.
CHOA KIM KEAT, Esq.

H. N. RIDLEY,
Honorary Secretary.

Rules

1. The competition shall be open to residents in Singapore, Penang, Malacca, and the Native States.

2. All articles exhibited for competition shall have been grown by the exhibitor, or must have been in his possession at least four weeks before the day of Exhibition—Bouquets and Table Decorations excepted.

3. It shall be distinctly understood that all plants exhibited in Section II. must be in flower, and fruits and vegetables must be fit for use.

4. All articles included in any entry must be arranged, and the exhibitors and assistants must finally leave the Hall, by noon on the day of the Exhibition.

5. The arrangement of the exhibits shall be subject to the directions of the Committee.

6. The Committee will appoint Judges, from whose decision there shall be no appeal.

7. The Judges will have authority to withhold the prize when they are of opinion that there is not sufficient merit to justify an award: or to award special prizes for anything not mentioned in the Schedule.

8. No Exhibitor shall be awarded two prizes in the same class, or more than five prizes in the same Section.

9. Intending Exhibitors are requested to give notice to the Honorary Secretary, at least five days before the day of the show, in what classes they intend to exhibit. On giving this

information they will receive numbered cards, which must be attached to the exhibits in place of the exhibitor's name.

10. No articles included in any entry shall be removed from the Hall before the close of the Show. Exhibitors will receive a ticket, marked with a number corresponding to that of their exhibits, which must be produced at the close of the Show before they can be removed.

If exhibitors will carefully attend to the Rules and Notes, and also label their productions with the numbers of the classes in which they wish them to be shown, confusion and trouble will be avoided.

All reasonable care will be taken of articles while on exhibition, but it must be distinctly understood that under no circumstances are the Committee liable for any damage that may occur.

SECTION I.—Ornamental Foliage Plants in Pots.

Class.	Kinds.	No. to be exhibited.	Prizes.	
			First $	Second $
1	Panax or Aralia	3	3	2
2	Coleus	6	3	2
3	,,	3	2	1
4	,,	specn.	1	...
5	Crotons	6	3	2
6	,,	3	2	1
7	,,	specn.	1	...
8	Maranta and Calathea	6	4	2
9	,, ,, ,,	3	3	1
10	,, ,, ,,	specn.	2	1
11	Palms	6	4	2
12	,,	3	3	1
13	Palm	specn.	2	...
14	Caladiums	6	3	2
15	,,	3	2	1
16	,,	specn.	2	
17	Dieffenbachias	3	2	
18	,,	specn.	1	
19	Aroids other than the above (Pothos, Sciudapsus, Alocasia, Colocasia, &c.)	6	4	2
20	,, ,,	3	3	1
21	,, ,,	specn.	3	...
22	Dracænas	3	2	...
23	,,	specn.	1	...
24	Ferns	12	7	3
25	,,	6	5	2
26	,,	3	5	2
27	Specimen Fern	...	3	...
28	Tree Fern	specn.	3	...
29	Selaginellas	6	4	2
30	,,	3	3	1
31	,,	specn.	2	...
32	Ornamental foliage plants not			
33	included in the above	3	3	2
34	Specimen	2	...	...
35	Heliconia	3	2	...
36	,,	specn.	1	...
37	Anthuriums	3	2	...
38	,,	specn.	1	..

SECTION II.—Plants in Pots, in Flower.

Class.	Kinds.	No. to be exhibited.	Prizes. First	Second
			$	$
39	Cannas	6	4	2
40	,,	3	3	1
41	,,	specn.	2	...
42	Eucharis		2	1
43	Geranium		2	1
44	Hibiscus	3	3	1
45	,,	specn.	2	1
46	Ixora	3	3	1
47	,,	specn.	2	1
48	Cockscombs		2	1
49	Dianthus (Pink)		2	1
50	Balsams		2	1
51	Zinnias		2	1
52	Roses	3	3	1
53	,,	specn.	2	1
54	Asters		2	1
55	Chrysanthemums		2	1
56	Dahlias		2	1
57	Phlox		2	1
58	Petunias		2	1
59	Antirrhinums (Snapdragon)		2	1
60	Gloxinias		4	2
61	,,	specn.	2	1
62	Other Gesneraceæ (Gesnera, Tydea, Achimenes, Episcia, &c.)		3	1
63	Verbenas		2	1
64	Gaillardias		2	1
65	Orchids	6	10	4
66	,,	3	5	2
67	,,	specn.	4	2
68	Amaryllids and Lilies		2	1
69	Plant in flower not included in above	specn.	3	
70	Best collection of different Plants in flower, not less than	12	10	5
71	Stephanotis	specn.	3	...

SECTION II.—PLANTS IN POTS, IN FLOWER—contd.

CLASS.	KINDS.	No. to be exhibited.	PRIZES.	
			First $	Second $
72	Marigold		2	1
73	Calliopsis		2	1
74	Sunflower		2	1

* For all classes in this Section, except classes in which the numbers are given and those denoted as specimens, the number of exhibits is not restricted, but in awarding prizes the judges will take into consideration the quantity as well as the quality of each exhibit.

Special prize for Rarest Orchid in show, $3.

SECTION III.—Plants in Pots, whether in Flower or not.

CLASS.	KINDS.	No. to be exhibited.	PRIZES.	
			First $	Second $
75	Begonias ...	12	5	3
76	,, ...	6	5	3
77	,, ...	3	3	2
78	,, ...	specn.	3	3
79	Succulents	3	3	2
80	,, ...	specn.	2	1
81	The rarest Native Plant ...		3	
82	,, Exotic ...		2	

SECTION IV.—Cut Flowers.

Class.	Kinds.	No. to be exhibited.	Prizes. First.	Second
			$	$
83	Dianthus	6	3	1
84	Zinnias	6	3	1
85	Roses Not less than	3	3	1
86	Gaillardias ,,	6	3	1
87	Asters ,,	6	3	1
88	Marigolds ,,	6	3	1
89	Chrysanthemums ,,	3	3	1
90	Calliopsis ,,	6	3	1
91	Dahlias ,,	3	3	1
92	Amaryllis or Lilies	3	3	1
93	Gardenias	3	3	1
94	Orchids	3	3	2
95	Ixoras	3	3	1
96	Stephanotis	3	3	1
97	Sunflowers	3	3	1
98	Buttonholes and Sprays ,,	4	3	1
99	Collection of Cut Flowers, arranged for effect	...	5	1
100	Cut Flowers, Specimens	6	3	2
101	Collection of Wild Flowers, arranged for effect	...	5	2
102	Hand Bouquet	...	4	1
103	Bridal ,, (White Flowers)	...	4	1
104	* Table Decoration	...	4	1

* The size of the Tables will be 10 feet by 4.

SECTION V.—Vegetables.

CLASS.	KINDS.	No. to be exhibited.	PRIZES.	
			First.	Second
			$	$
105	Carrots ...	6	1	0 50
106	Cucumbers	4	1	0 50
107	Brinjal	4	1	0 50
108	Lettuces	4	1	0 50
109	French Beans ...	20 pds.	1	0 50
110	Peas	20 pds.	1	0 50
111	Onions or Shallots	12	1	0 50
112	Radishes	12	1	0 50
113	Tomatoes	6	1	0 50
114	Cabbages	2	1	0 50
115	Vegetable Marrows	2	1	0 50
116	Sweet Potato (Kledi)	12	1	
117	,, ,, (Yam) ...	12	1	...
118	Celery...	3 stalks	1	0 50
119	Beet-root	3	1	0 50
120	Artichokes	6	1	0 50
121	Chillies...	6	1	0 50
122	Collection of European Vegetables	...	5	...
123	Collection of Native Vegetables		3	1 00
124	Any Vegetable not included in the above	...	1	0 50

SECTION VI.—Fruits.

Class.	Kinds.	No. to be exhibited.	Prizes.	
			First. $	Second $
125	Melons	2	2	1
126	Oranges	12	2	1
127	Limes (including Lemons and Citron)	12	2	1
128	Pumelows	2	2	1
129	Pine Apples	3	2	1
130	Durians	2	3	1
131	Plantains (different sorts)	...	2	1
132	Mangosteens	12	2	1
133	Sour Sops	3	2	1
134	Custard Apples	3	2	1
135	Chikus	2	2	1
136	Collection of Fruit	...	3	1

SECTION VII.—Miscellaneous.

Class.	Kinds.	No. to be exhibited.	Prizes.	
			First.	Second
137	Tapioca Roots	6	1	
138	Arrowroots	6	1	
139	Ginger Roots	6	1	
140	Turmeric ...	6	1	
141	Cocoa-nuts (ripe)	6	2	
142	Cacao Fruits	6	2	
143	Nutmegs ...	12	2	
144	Collection of Spices ...		2	
145	Sugar Cane ...		1	
146	Pepper, sample of fresh ...		1	
147	Arabian Coffee		2	
148	Liberian Coffee ...		2	
149	Tea ...		2	
150	Collection of Chinese Plants, in pots, of fantastic shape ...		2	1
151	Other vegetable products not included in above	...	2	

PRIZE LIST

OF THE

FLOWER SHOW

TO BE HELD IN THE

TOWN HALL,

ON

Tuesday the 29th March, 1898.

Open from 4 p.m. to 6.30 p.m. & 8 to 11 p.m.
Admission, each person - - - $1
Family Ticket - - - - - $3

H. N. RIDLEY,

Honorary Secretary.

Singapore:
Printed at "The Sin Yew Hean" Press.

COMMITTEE.

St. V. B. Down, Esq.   W. Coveney, Esq.

R. Little, Esq.   R. H. Padday, Esq.

A. P. Adams, Esq.   Choa Kim Keat, Esq.

C. Stringer, Esq.

                                      H. N. RIDLEY,

                                          Honorary Secretary.

Rules.

1. The competition shall be open to residents in Singapore, Penang, Malacca, and the Native States.

2. All articles exhibited for competition shall have been grown by the exhibitor, or must have been in his possession at least four weeks before the day of Exhibition—Bouquets and Table Decorations excepted.

3. It shall be distinctly understood that all plants exhibited in Section II. must be in flower and distinct varieties.

4. All articles included in any entry must be arranged, and the exhibitors and assistants must finally leave the Hall, by noon on the day of the Exhibition.

5. The arrangement of the exhibits shall be subject to the directions of the Committee.

6. The Committee will appoint Judges, from whose decision there shall be no appeal.

7. The Judges will have authority to withhold the prize when they are of opinion that there is not sufficient merit to justify an award: or to award special prizes for anything not mentioned in the Schedule.

8. No Exhibitor shall be awarded two prizes in the same class, or more than five prizes in the same Section.

9. Intending Exhibitors are requested to give notice to the Honorary Secretary, at least five days before the day of the show, in what classes they intend to exhibit.

On giving this information they will receive numbered cards, which must be attached to the exhibits in place of the exhibitor's name.

10. No articles included in any entry shall be removed from the Hall before the close of the Show. Exhibitors will receive a ticket, marked with a number corresponding to that of their exhibits, which must be produced at the close of the Show before they can be removed.

If exhibitors will carefully attend to the Rules and Notes, and also label their productions with the numbers of the classes in which they wish them to be shown, confusion and trouble will be avoided.

All reasonable care will be taken of articles while on exhibition, but it must be distinctly understood that under no circumstances are the Committee liable for any damage that may occur.

SECTION I.—Ferns and Selaginellas.

Class.		No. to be exhibited.	Prizes.	
			1st. $	2nd. $
1	Ferns	12	10	5
2	,,	6	7	3
3	,,	3	7	3
4	,, Specimen	...	5	...
5	Selaginellas	6	7	3
6	,,	3	7	3
7	,, specimen	...	5	...

SECTION II.—Plants in Flower.

Class.		No. to be exhibited.	Prizes.	
			1st. $	2nd. $
8	Orchids	12	15	10
9	,,	6	10	5
10	,,	3	5	3
11	,, specimen	...	10	
12	,, rarest orchid in show	...	10	...
13	Gloxinias	6	4	2

SECTION II.—Plants in Flower—contd.

Class.		No. to be exhibited.	Prizes.	
			1st. $	2nd. $
14	Gloxinias	3	3	2
15	,, specimen	...	3	...
16	Chrysanthemums	3	3	2
17	,, specimen	...	2	...
18	Dahlias ...	6	4	2
19	,, specimen	...	2	...
20	Roses	3	4	2
21	,, specimen...	...	2	...
22	Cannas ...	6	5	3
23	,, ...	3	3	2
24	,, specimen	...	3	...
25	Eucharis specimen	...	2	...
26	Amaryllis and Lilies	3	3	2
27	,, specimen ...	...	2	...
28	Hibiscus...	3	3	2
29	,, specimen	...	2	...
30	Ixoras ...	3	3	2
31	,, specimen...	...	2	...
32	Stephanotis, specimen	...	3	...
33	Cockcombs not less than	3	2	1
34	Dianthus (Pinks) ,,	3	2	1

SECTION II.—PLANTS IN FLOWER—contd.

CLASS.		No. to be exhibited.	PRIZES.	
			1ST. $	2ND. $
35	Balsams not less than	3	2	1
36	Zinnias ,,	3	2	1
37	Asters ,,	3	2	1
38	Phlox ,,	3	2	1
39	Petunias ,,	3	2	1
40	Antirrhinums (Snap-dragons) not less than ...	3	2	1
41	Other Gesneraceæ—Achimenes, Episcia, Tydea &c	3	2	1
42	Verbenas not less than	3	2	1
43	Gaillardias ,,	3	2	1
44	Best Collection of Distinct Annuals ...	12	5	3
45	,, ...	6	4	2
46	Best collection of different Plants in flower ...	12	10	5
47	,, ,, ...	6	5	3
48	,, ,, specimen	...	4	...
49	Rarest Malayan plant in flower		5	
50	Rarest Exotic plant in flower	...	5	...

SECTION III.—Plants whether in flower or not.

Class.		No. to be exhibited.	Prizes.	
			1st. $	2nd. $
51	Begonias	12	10	5
52	,,	6	7	3
53	,,	3	7	3
54	,, specimen		5	...

SECTION IV.—Cut Flowers.

Class.		No. to be exhibited.	Prizes.	
			1st. $	2nd. $
55	Roses distinct varieties	3	2	1
56	Chrysanthemums ,,	3	2	1
57	Dahlias ,,	3	2	1
58	Cannas ,,	3	2	1
59	Orchids ,,	3	2	1
60	Amaryllis & Lilies ,,	3	2	1
61	Gardenias not less than	3	2	1
62	Stephanotis spray	....	2	1
63	Ixoras not less than	3	2	1
64	Hibiscus ,,	3	2	1

SECTION IV.—CUT FLOWERS—contd.

Class.		No. to be exhibited.	Prizes.	
			1st. $	2nd. $
65	Collection of Annuals distinct kinds	12	4	2
66	Collection of Annuals ...	6	2	1
67	Collection of cut flowers arranged for effect ...		5	2
68	Collection of wild flowers arranged for effect ...		5	2
69	Button-holes & sprays ...	4	3	1
70	Hand Bouquet		4	1
71	Bridal ,, white flowers		4	1
72	* Table decoration		10	5

* Size of tables will be 10' × 4' supplied by Committee.

PRIZE LIST

OF THE

FLOWER SHOW

TO BE HELD IN THE

TOWN HALL,

ON

Tuesday, the 11th April, 1899.

Open from 4 p.m. to 6.30 p.m. & 8 to 11 p.m.

Admission, each person   -   -   - $1.

H. N. RIDLEY,
Honorary Secretary.

Singapore:

Printed at "The Sin Yew Hean" Press.

COMMITTEE.

St. V. B. Down, Esq.   Col: Pennefather,

C. Stringer, Esq.   W. Nanson, Esq.

R. H. Padday, Esq.   E. J. Khory, Esq.

H. N. RIDLEY,
Honorary Secretary.

Rules.

1. The competition shall be open to residents in Singapore, Penang, Malacca, and the Native States.

2. All articles exhibited for competition shall have been grown by the exhibitor, or must have been in his possession at least four weeks before the day of Exhibition—Bouquets and Table Decorations excepted.

3. It shall be distinctly understood that all plants exhibited in Section II. must be in flower and distinct varieties.

4. All articles included in any entry must be arranged, and the exhibitors and assistants must finally leave the Hall, by noon on the day of the Exhibition.

5. The arrangement of the exhibits shall be subject to the directions of the Committee.

6. The Committee will appoint Judges, from whose decision there shall be no appeal.

7. The Judges will have authority to withhold the prize when they are of opinion that there is not sufficient merit to justify an award ; or to award special prizes for anything not mentioned in the Schedule.

8. No Exhibitor shall be awarded two prizes in the same class, or more than five prizes in the same Section.

9. Intending Exhibitors are requested to give notice to the Honorary Secretary, at least five days before the day of the show, in what classes they intend to exhibit. On giving

this information they will receive numbered cards, which must be attached to the exhibits in place of the exhibitor's name.

10. No articles included in any entry shall be removed from the Hall before the close of the Show. Exhibitors will receive a ticket, marked with a number corresponding to that of their exhibits, which must be produced at the close of the Show before they can be removed.

If exhibitors will carefully attend to the Rules and Notes and also label their productions with the numbers of the classes in which they wish them to be shown, confusion and trouble will be avoided.

All reasonable care will be taken of articles while on exhibition, but it must be distinctly understood that under no circumstances are the Committee liable for any damage that may occur.

SECTION I.—Ferns and Selaginellas.

Class.		No. to be exhibited.	Prizes.	
			1st. $	2nd. $
1	Ferns	12	10	5
2	,,	6	7	3
3	,,	3	7	3
4	,, Specimen	...	5	...
5	Selaginellas	6	7	3
6	,,	3	7	3
7	,, specimen	...	5	...

SECTION II.—Plants in Flower.

Class.		No. to be exhibited.	Prizes.	
			1st. $	2nd. $
8	Orchids	12	15	10
9	,,	6	10	5
10	,,	3	5	3
11	,, specimen	...	10	...
12	,, rarest orchid in show	...	10	...
13	Gloxinias	6	4	2

SECTION II.—PLANTS IN FLOWER—contd.

Class.		No. to be exhibited.	Prizes.	
			1st. $	2nd. $
14	Gloxinias	3	3	2
15	,, specimen	...	3	...
16	Chrysanthemums	3	3	2
17	,, specimen	...	2	...
18	Dahlias ...	6	4	2
19	,, specimen	...	2	...
20	Roses	3	4	2
21	,, specimen ...	...	2	...
22	Cannas ...	6	5	3
23	,,	3	3	2
24	,, specimen	...	3	...
25	Eucharis specimen	...	2	...
26	Amaryllis and Lilies	3	3	2
27	,, specimen ...	...	2	...
28	Hibiscus ...	3	3	2
29	,, specimen	...	2	...
30	Ixoras ...	3	3	2
31	,, specimen ...	...	2	...
32	Stephanotis, specimen ...	...	3	...
33	Cockcombs not less than	3	2	1
34	Dianthus (Pinks) ,.	3	2	1

SECTION II.—Plants in Flower—contd.

Class.		No. to be exhibited	Prizes.	
			1st. $	2nd. $
35	Balsams not less than	3	2	1
36	Zinnias ,,	3	2	1
37	Asters ,,	3	2	1
38	Phlox ,,	3	2	1
39	Petunias ,,	3	2	1
40	Antirrhinums (Snap-dragons) not less than	3	2	1
41	Other Gesneraceæ-Archimenes, Episcia, Tydea, &c.	3	2	1
42	Verbenas not less than	3	2	1
43	Gaillardias ,,	3	2	1
44	Best Collection of Distinct Annuals	12	5	3
45	,, ...	6	4	2
46	Best collection of different Plants in flower ...	12	10	5
47	,, ,, ...	6	5	3
48	,, ,, specimen	..	4	...
49	Rarest Malayan plant in flower ...		5	...
50	Rarest Exotic plant in flower		5	...

SECTION III.—Plants whether in flower or not.

Class.		No. to be exhibited.	Prizes.	
			1st. $	2nd. $
51	Begonias ...	12	10	5
52	,,	6	7	3
53	,, ...	3	7	3
54	,, specimen ...		5	...

SECTION IV.—Cut Flowers.

Class.		No. to be exhibited.	Prizes.	
			1st. $	2nd. $
55	Roses distinct varieties	3	2	1
56	Chrysanthemums ,,	3	2	1
57	Dahlias ,,	3	2	1
58	Cannas ,,	3	2	1
59	Orchids ,,	3	2	1
60	Amaryllis & Lilies ,,	3	2	1
61	Gardenias not less than	3	2	1
62	Stephanotis spray ...	...	2	1
63	Ixoras not less than ...	3	2	1
64	Hibiscus ,,	3	2	1

SECTION IV.—CUT FLOWERS—contd.

Class.		No. to be exhibited.	Prizes.	
			1st. $	2nd. $
65	Collection of Annuals distinct kinds	12	4	2
66	Collection of Annuals	6	2	1
67	Collection of cut flowers arranged for effect ...	..	5	2
68	Collection of wild flowers arranged for effect ...	...	5	2
69	Button-holes & sprays ...	4	3	1
70	Hand Bouquet		4	1
71	Bridal ,, white flowers		4	1
72	* Table decoration	....	10	5

* Size of tables will be 10' × 4' supplied by Committee.

PRIZE LIST

OF THE

FLOWER SHOW

TO BE HELD IN THE

TOWN HALL

On Tuesday, the 10th April, 1900.

Open from 4 P.M. to 6.30 P.M. and 8 to 11 P.M.

ADMISSION, each person $1

H. N RIDLEY,.
Honorary Secretary.

SINGAPORE:
Printed at "The YU SHING" Press.

COMMITTEE.

St. V. B. Down, Esq.   Col: Pennefather.

Hon: C. Stringer,   E. J. Khory, Esq.

Choa Kim Keat   *J. E. Jap*

                                    H. N. Ridley,

                                          Honorary Secretary.

RULES.

1. The competition shall be open to residents in Singapore, Penang, Malacca, and the Native States.

2. All articles exhibited for competition shall have been grown by the exhibitor, or must have been in his possession at least four weeks before the day of exhibition—Bouquets and Table Decorations excepted.

3. It shall be distinctly understood that all plants exhibited in Section II. must be in flower and distinct varieties.

4. All articles included in any entry must be arranged and the exhibitors and assistants must finally leave the Hall by noon on the day of the Exhibition.

5. The arrangement of the exhibits shall be subject to the directions of the Committee.

6. The Committee will appoint Judges, from whose decision there shall be no appeal.

7. The Judges will have authority to withhold the prize when they are of opinion that there is not sufficient merit to justify an award : or to award special prizes for anything not mentioned in the Schedule.

8. No Exhibitor shall be awarded two prizes in the same class, or more than five prizes in the same Section.

9. Intending Exhibitors are requested to give notice to the Honorary Secretary, at least five days before the day of the show, in what classes they intend to exhibit. On giving

this information they will receive numbered cards, which must be attached to the exhibits in place of the exhibitor's name.

10. No articles included in any entry shall be removed from the Hall before the close of the Show. Exhibitors will receive a ticket, marked with a number corresponding to that of their exhibits, which must be produced at the close of the show before they can be removed.

If exhibitors will carefully attend to the Rules and Notes and also label their productions with the numbers of the classes in which they wish them to be shown, confusion and trouble will be avoided.

All reasonable care will be taken of articles while on exhibition, but it must be distinctly understood that under no circumstances are the Committee liable for any damage that may occur.

Section I.—Ferns and Selaginellas.

Class.		No to be exhibited.	Prizes.	
			1st $	2nd $
1	Ferns	12	10	5
2	,, ...	6	7	3
3	,, ...	3	7	3
4	,, Specimen ...	...	5	...
5	Selaginellas	6	7	3
6	,, ...	3	7	3
7	,, specimen ...	...	5	...

Section II—.Plants in Flower.

Class.		No. to be exhibited.	Prizes.	
			1st. $	2nd. $
8	Orchids	12	15	10
9	,, ...	6	10	5
10	,, ...	3	5	3
11	,, specimen ...	.	10	..
12	,, rarest orchid in show... ...	..	10	...
13	Gloxinias	6	4	2

Section II.— Plants in Flower—contd.

CLASS.		No. to be exhibited.	PRIZES.	
			1ST $	2ND $
14	Gloxinias	3	3	2
15	„ specimen ...	...	3	...
16	Chrysanthemums ...	3	3	2
17	„ specimen	...	2	...
18	Dahlias	6	4	2
19	„ specimen ...		2	
20	Roses	3	4	2
21	„ specimen ...		2	...
22	Cannas	6	5	3
23	„	3	3	2
24	„ specimen ...		3	...
25	Eucharis specimen ...		2	...
26	Amaryllis and Lilies ...	3	3	2
27	„ specimen ...	...	2	...
28	Hibiscus...	3	8	2
29	„ specimen ...	...	2	..
30	Ixoras	3	3	2
31	„ specimen ...	...	2	...
32	Stephanotis, specimen ...	...	3	...
33	Cockcombs not less than	3	2	1
34	Dianthus (Pink „	3	2	1

Section II.—Plants in Flower—*Contd.*

CLASS.		No. to be exhibited.	PRIZES.	
			1ST. $	2ND. $
35	Balsams not less than	3	2	1
36	Zinnias ,,	3	2	1
37	Asters ,,	3	2	1
38	Phlox ,,	3	2	1
39	Petunias ,,	3	2	1
40	Antirrhinums (Snap-dragons) not less than	3	2	1
41	Other Gesneraceæ-Achimenes, Episcia, Tydea, &c	3	2	1
42	Verbenas not less than	3	2	1
43	Gaillardias ,,	3	2	1
44	Best Collection of Distinct Annuals	12	5	3
45	,, ...	6	4	2
46	Best collection of different Plants in flower ...	12	10	5
47	,, ,, ...	6	5	3
48	,, ,, specimen	..	4	...

Section III.—Plants whether in Flower or not.

Class.		No to be exhibited.	Prizes.	
			1st. $	2nd. $
49	Rarest Malayan plant		5	...
50	Rarest Exotic plant	...	5	...
51	Begonias	6	7	3
52	,, ...	3	7	3
53	,, specimen ...	...	5	
54	Dracænas	6	5	3
55	,, ...	3	3	
56	,, specimen ...	...	3	
57	Caladium	3	5	
58	,, ...	3	3	...
59	,, specimen ...	...	3	...

Section IV.—Cut Flowers.

Class.		No. to be exhibited.	Prizes.	
			1st. $	2nd. $
60	Roses distinct varieties	3	2	1
61	Chrysanthemums ,,	3	2	1
62	Dahlias ,,	3	2	1
63	Cannas ,,	3	2	1

Section IV.—Cut Flowers—contd.

CLASS.		No. to be exhibited.	PRIZES.	
			1ST. $	2ND $
64	Orchids ,,	3	2	1
65	Amaryllis & Lilies ,,	3	2	1
66	Gardenias not less than	3	2	1
67	Stephanotis spray	3	2	1
68	Ixoras not less than		2	1
69	Hibiscus not less than	3	2	1
70	Collection of Annuals distinct kinds	12	4	1
71	Collection of Annuals	6	2	2
72	Collection of cut flowers arranged for effect		5	2
73	Collection of wild flowers arranged for effect		5	2
74	Button-holes & sprays	4	3	1
75	Hand Bouquet		4	1
76	Bridal ,, white flower		4	1
77	* Table decoration.		10	5

* Size of tables will be 10' X 4' supplied by Committee.

www.ingramcontent.com/pod-product-compliance
Lightning Source LLC
Chambersburg PA
CBHW032142160426
43197CB00008B/744